The Veil of Dreams and Reality

Betty Duncan-Göetz

Order this book online at www.trafford.com/06-0307
or email orders@trafford.com

Most Trafford titles are also available at major online book retailers.

Note for Librarians: A cataloguing record for this book is available from Library and Archives Canada at www.collectionscanada.ca/amicus/index-e.html

ISBN: 978-1-4120-8551-9

We at Trafford believe that it is the responsibility of us all, as both individuals and corporations, to make choices that are environmentally and socially sound. You, in turn, are supporting this responsible conduct each time you purchase a Trafford book, or make use of our publishing services. To find out how you are helping, please visit www.trafford.com/responsiblepublishing.html

Our mission is to efficiently provide the world's finest, most comprehensive book publishing service, enabling every author to experience success. To find out how to publish your book, your way, and have it available worldwide, visit us online at www.trafford.com/10510

www.trafford.com

North America & international
toll-free: 1 888 232 4444 (USA & Canada)
phone: 250 383 6864 ♦ fax: 250 383 6804 ♦ email: info@trafford.com

The United Kingdom & Europe
phone: +44 (0)1865 722 113 ♦ local rate: 0845 230 9601
facsimile: +44 (0)1865 722 868 ♦ email: info.uk@trafford.com

10 9 8 7 6

CONTENTS

Where we love is home,
home that our feet may leave,
but not our hearts.

Oliver Wendell Holmes

The Home Place,
Ashland, KY

CHAPTER ONE

Family Matters – 1927

THE CHILD lay on her back, her dark wavy hair spread across the pillow. Her blue-gray eyes were open, and she stared up at the ceiling. But she did not see the cracks in the plaster, nor feel the breeze as it gently pushed the blue flowered curtains in and out of the small window. Nor, did she hear the family talking from the kitchen where breakfast was being prepared. Her small body was tense and covered with perspiration. Above her swirled a mass of smoke and flames. She heard horses stamping in terror from the old red barn. Beside the large porch veranda of the two story farm house a giant pine tree caught fire and flamed up like a great torch, throwing smoke and sparks as it danced in its death song. The rope swing that hung in the tree blazed up and curled snake-like and fell to the ground. The child trembled and shivered with dread. She knew this house and the red barn. She loved the horses and the old house, now completely engulfed in flames. It was the home of her Aunt Charlotte!

• 2

A soundless scream came deep inside the child's throat and she fell into a swoon-like faint. The terrible "vision" faded from her consciousness and as it faded she gradually became aware that her sister, Maggie, was calling her. She tried to answer but her voice would not come. Maggie came into the child's room. She intended to scold her, but when she saw Becka's pale face, she realized that she was very upset. Sitting down on the small bed, she gathered her little sister into her arms and soothed her with quiet cooing sounds. Becka's little body gradually relaxed and she smiled faintly up at her big sister, putting her small arms around Maggie and snuggling close.

"You've had one of your bad dreams, haven't you honey?" she softly asked the little girl.

Becka nodded. "Yes," she said, her voice small and frightened. Maggie helped Becka dress and the two girls went down the long center hall to the kitchen where their mother, Elizabeth was preparing breakfast. When Elizabeth looked at Becka she knew immediately that Becka had had another of her "terrible dreams." She dried her hands on her apron and stooped to pick up the little girl.

"Oh Mama!" cried Becka, "You must call Aunt Charlotte right now. You must, you must!"

"I will, child, but first we'll have some breakfast, then I promise to call Charlotte right away."

"Please don't wait, Mama, please," Becka begged. Elizabeth sighed and picked up the wall phone. She rang her sister Charlotte's number. It was a long-distance call, as Charlotte lived fifty miles out in the country.

"Hello" came the answer, and Elizabeth could tell that Charlotte was agitated.

"Hello Charlotte, is everything alright?" Elizabeth asked, suddenly feeling very uneasy.

"No, I'm sorry Sis, I can't talk now. The horses are stamping and calling out in the barn, the dog's barking and I smell smoke. I'm sorry, I'll have to see what's going on." And the phone went dead.

As Charlotte turned from the telephone, she heard a loud crackling sound coming from the upper part of their house. She started to climb the stairs but the collie dog blocked her way, barking and pushing her back down the steps. When they reached the bottom landing, smoke curled out of the stairwell causing Charlotte to choke and cough. She and the collie ran out onto the front veranda and looked frantically around for her husband, Frank. Then she saw him along, with their youngest son at the barn. They were leading the horses outside into the meadow.

"Charlotte," Frank called to her. "What is it? What's all that smoke?"

"Oh, Frank, the house is on fire!" she screamed.

Frank and their son, Charles, ran up the long driveway to the house. But by the time they reached the veranda and the front door, the entire interior was engulfed in flames. They could not enter. The smoke and flames were so intense that they were driven back into the yard.

Neighbors, who were passing by, ran quickly to help. All the livestock was led safely to the meadow, and a bucket line was formed to throw water from the old well onto the side of the barn nearest the house. The labor was back – breaking, but no one gave up. The barn was saved but the beautiful old two-story farmhouse that had stood there for over 100 years was burned to the ground!

Lost! Everything was lost. All the beautiful quilts, hand made with such loving fingers. The blue Willow china, the old pictures on the walls, the photograph albums, the baby grand piano that Becka loved to play….all gone. Now just a pile of burned cinders, smoldering with the putrid smell of destruction.

Meanwhile, in Ashland, Elizabeth finished up the breakfast dishes. She reached for the telephone and tried to call her sister again, but the line was dead. Her heart filled with dread. Taking off her apron she said to Ben, her husband that she wanted to go out to Charlotte's home right away. Becka begged to go too, for the dream was haunting her. At first Elizabeth refused, saying that the child should stay home with Maggie. However, Maggie wanted to go also, so Elizabeth finally piled all the family into the big Packard and they set off for the country.

And after the fire a sound of sheer silence.

1 Kings 19:12

When the family arrived at the farm, it was to a scene of almost total despair. Charlotte, Frank and young Charles were in a state of shock. They had lost everything they owned, everything but the outbuildings and the livestock. As the big Packard pulled into the long dirt and gravel driveway, young Charles ran to meet them. The family climbed out of the car, and stared in dismay at the ruins of the beautiful old home. Becka burst into tears, and ran to Charlotte, sobbing and holding on to her aunt's skirts. Charlotte stooped down and enfolded the little girl in her arms.

"Don't cry, honey. It can be replaced, and we are all safe," she whispered to her little niece.

"If only I had known sooner, if only, if only," cried Becka, and her body shook with her sobs.

Elizabeth, witnessing the whole scene, turned to her husband, Benjamin. "Oh Ben, what are we going to do about Becka? Those terrible 'dreams' are killing her. She's a nervous wreck, feeling that these awful things that happen are somehow her fault, for not 'telling about them' sooner." Ben shook his head.

At a loss as to what to do about his little daughter, Ben simply shook his head. So precious to him, he loved this tiny child with all his heart and wanted only the happiest times for her. Yet he knew that there was something so very different and unusual about her.

She was not at all like her sister. Maggie, the oldest daughter, was so down to earth, practical and levelheaded, with a "no-nonsense" attitude. Bart, an older son who had been killed in an accident, had been very close to Becka. He had had a loving, quiet though withdrawn nature, and Ben was often at a loss to know how to approach the boy.

Ben recalled that Becka had had one of her "dreams" shortly before Bart was killed. She had clung to Bart and begged him not to ride his motorcycle that morning. "Stay home with me, today," Becka had begged. But Bart had only laughed, and hugged his little sister and assured her he would be home soon to read her another story. Bart never read to Becka again. Shortly after he roared out of the driveway on his motorcycle he crashed into the rear of a slow moving truck…and instantly killed.

Becka had been devastated, as were the rest of the family. However, Becka's grief was so profound, that she had to be sedated. She was only four years old at the time and seemed older than her years. She and Bart had spent long hours together, reading and playing special games that they both enjoyed, games of make-believe, magic and wonderful times of closeness and fun. Bart had been drawn to Becka from the time she was an infant. He had felt a special bond with the child, and often relieved his mother of her care by taking her for long walks, and caring for her as lovingly as his mother cared for her. William, the third child, always called Will, had tried to fill the loss of Bart by keeping close to Becka, but it had not helped her broken heart.

Ben remembered all these things as he pondered his wife's question. He knew not what to say or do about his little daughter and her strange "dreams." Meanwhile, Charlotte tried to console Becka by telling her that the mother cat, Millie, had saved herself and her five kittens from the burning kitchen. Somehow, she had sensed the danger, and had taken the kittens out the side door to a safe place beneath some bushes. Young Charles had found her, singed but healthy, with all her brood intact.

Becka was able to smile at this good news, and ran with Charles to the little family of kittens. She picked them up and held them close, with Millie looking on in approval. While the children were occupied, the adults were inspecting the barn and the out buildings.

"I think the barn can be made livable," Frank said. "We can stay there until we rebuild the house. It won't be easy, but I think we can pull it off." When Ben started to protest, Frank continued. "I know, I know, we could move in with you, but we need to be here to supervise the building, and to take care of the animals and, well, the whole place," he said with finality.

And that was how it was settled. The neighbors and the family members pitched in with bed clothing, towels, and all the necessities for living in an old barn. The hay mounds were transformed into makeshift beds. The pump was fixed with a pipe that ran to the front stall of the barn, and a make do kitchen was installed.

Pots and pans, dishes and flatware were appearing, as neighbors and friends raided their own kitchens in order to help in any way possible. The local church members obtained clothing for the whole family from donations and it seemed that as if by magic the old barn was transformed into a "home."

For young Charles and Frank, Jr. it was a grand adventure. Living in a barn was fun and full of excitement! Becka's brothers, Will, and the twins Harry and Henry were actually jealous of their cousins Charles and Frank. They agreed that living in a barn was really great!

Charlotte, however, did not find the arrangement so much "fun." It was hard going for her, as she got little rest at night. She had been used to soft beds and convenience in cooking. She mourned her beautiful old home, so convenient and roomy. At night when she was alone, she wept for her many lost treasures, especially the photographs of her family, the baby photos, and the small mementos she had saved over the years: the school treasures of her children, the precious hand-made quilts, and the crocheted shawls, made by Sarah, her mother.

Charlotte's husband, Dr. Franklin Mason was the only rural doctor for miles around. He soon had fashioned a place in the barn to see his patients. Those who could come to him. However, he saw most of his patients on his daily rounds. He was so thankful that his medical bag and some of his most used medicines had not been in the house when it burned.

Ben, who was an excellent electrician, had wired in a new telephone at the barn. This enabled Frank's many patients to reach him if necessary. His medical practice and the overseeing of the work on the rebuilding kept Frank very busy all day long. He was usually so tired that when he went to bed, it did not matter where he slept. He was asleep as soon as his head hit the pillow, even if the pillow was filled with straw!

The building went smoothly and quickly. There were

many hands to help. Benjamin and Elizabeth came often with food and other items that were needed. Will and the twins helped in many ways, carrying supplies and being "gophers" for their Uncle Frank. Neighbor men who were skilled in construction came to help, and before many weeks passed, a new house began to take shape. Frank, who had always been careful to save "for a rainy day," had enough saved to buy the materials needed, and to compensate the workers. He was very glad he had kept his money in the bank, and not at home as some of his neighbors did.

When the final windows and doors were in place, when the final nail had been struck, Charlotte and Frank called everyone together who had been a part of building process. There was to be a grand outdoor picnic.

The children were excited and organized games and contests; games of hide and seek, and blind man's bluff. The picnic tables were laden with delicious food: mounds of fried chicken, fried potatoes and whipped potatoes, juicy ripe tomatoes, and green beans cooked with bacon and mushrooms, and ham and roast beef. There were so many pies and cakes: apple, peach, strawberry-rhubarb pies and angel food cake and gold cake.

There was even homemade ice cream from the hand cranked ice cream maker that Elizabeth brought from her home. Becka and her twin brothers, Henry and Harry had taken turns at the crank, turning and turning until it became stiff and the ice cream was ready to eat.

The weather cooperated with a bright, sunny day. All agreed that the building of the new home was a great success, and the outdoor picnic was the best of all! There were smiles on every face that night, and even Charlotte fell asleep without her usual turning and twisting.

Tomorrow, they would be sleeping in their new home!

She was exhausted, but felt happy and content. The next morning the furniture arrived from Huntington. There were two large horse-drawn wagons full of furniture, and everything seemed to be in good shape. Ben, Elizabeth and their children and some of the neighbors helped carry the furniture into the house. What a joy it was to Charlotte to see the house take shape.

The new house could never quite take the place of the old home that burned, but it was still wonderful to Charlotte, to be able to move into a home again! She and Elizabeth had fun arranging and re-arranging everything, until Frank threw up his hands and walked outside, shaking his head.

"I give up," he said to Ben, laughing, and the two men walked down to the barn to look over the livestock.

The horses had been uneasy and skittish during the time the family had occupied their "space" and King the golden collie dog had walked around looking confused and troubled. The cow and the pigs took everything in stride and did not seem to mind the change. Where their humans slept was of no concern to them. As long as their humans fed them, they were happy.

Ben reached down and patted the collie. "Don't worry old fellow," he said. "You'll soon be back in your old barn and your own bed."

"He's been real bent out of shape since we moved into the barn," remarked Frank. "Somehow our being there didn't set with his sense of propriety. He just felt the barn was no place for his humans." Both men laughed, and Frank gave the dog a warm tousle of his head. King wagged his tail and licked Frank's hand. Apparently all was as it should be again.

"You know, Ben, this dog saved Charlotte's life. If he hadn't stopped her from climbing those stairs, well I don't want to think about it," Frank said.

"I know," said Ben. Then he looked at Frank with a quizzical expression. "Did Charlotte tell you about Becka's dream?" He asked, questioningly.

"Yes, she did. I don't know what to tell you, Ben. The child is – how shall I say it – a bit unusual?" And he shook his head.

"You're a doctor, Frank. What do you think we should do about the child?"

"I just don't know, Ben. I am not that kind of a doctor. Perhaps you should take her to a specialist, someone who knows more than I do about this sort of thing. I mean, someone who has had training in this field," Frank said, pulling his mustache.

Ben was silent for a long time. Frank seemed to be at a loss for anything else to suggest. "Where would I find such a doctor? I don't know if I ever heard of anyone around these parts," Ben asked, with a troubled look.

"I can get you the address and phone number of a clinic in New York," Frank said. "They may help. However, they would probably want to keep Becka there for observation. That would be very traumatic for her."

Frank shook his head and pulled at his mustache, thinking that leaving so young a child all alone would be very hard for the family as well as little Becka, not to mention the cost.

Ben shook his head and rammed his fists into his pockets. "Well, maybe she will grow out of it."

"That is possible," answered Frank. Both men were doubtful, but did not want to voice their doubts. Frank, as a doctor, knew that these things had a tendency to get worse, not better. They continued to discuss the problem, along with other concerns, until they were called to the house for dinner. They went to dinner with relief. It was a thorny problem, this problem of Becka, and they were glad to lay it aside for now.

By the time Ben and Elizabeth had gathered the children and driven the fifty miles to their home, it was quite dark, and the children went quickly to bed. However, Ben and Elizabeth talked until the wee hours of the morning. If they took Becka to New York to the clinic, neighbors would talk. Things like that could not be kept secret in such a small town where everyone knew everyone else.

They finally decided to talk to Becka to somehow make her understand that her "dreams" should be kept strictly in the family, that she tell no one about them except family members. Also, the family would be told to keep these things inside the family. No one should talk about this to anyone else, no teachers, playmates, neighbors or even best friends. Elizabeth and Ben also wanted to explain to the whole extended family, as well as Becka, that these "dreams" came to Becka without her asking, and Becka was in no way responsible for them. They came unbidden and unsought.

After breakfast the next day, the family had a meeting where everyone gathered. The older children knew that it was important, and sat solemnly listening. Becka sat on her mother's lap. She trembled slightly, realizing that the "meeting" was about her. Elizabeth hugged the child and gave her a kiss on the cheek. Then she outlined the plan for the rest of the family. After she finished, she turned to each one, to see if they fully understood. Then she asked Becka if she understood the importance of keeping her "dreams" for the family, only. The child nodded slowly, and whispered, "Yes, Mommy, I understand."

Liz

CHAPTER TWO

Strength and dignity are her clothing,
And she laughs at the time to come.

Proverbs 31: 25

Elizabeth – 1885

ELIZABETH EUREKA Seagraves was born in the small town of Paintsville, Kentucky, December 13, 1885. She was the fifth child in a family of seven children, growing up on a farm in Kentucky at a time when large families were commonplace.

All of the children worked on the farm. Liz, as the family called her, did her share of the work. Washing and mending clothes, hoeing in the garden, cleaning the chicken coops (a job she detested), and doing all of the other chores her mother assigned.

However, it was not all work for Liz and her younger sister Lou. They had plenty of time to play with their dolls, make them clothes, build playhouses under the large old oak trees, and ride the horses around the sixty-acre farm. Sometimes on a Sunday afternoon the children thrilled to watch their mother and father race their horses around the track in back of the barn. For these were not work horses, these animals were beautiful. Oh, on occasion they might pull the family's pretty little buggy back and forth to church, but for the most part these horses were for riding.

And it was a thrilling sight; Sarah and Green, neck in neck, racing over the broad pastures as fast as the horses could carry them. And, unsurprisingly, Sarah's long hair would inevitably come loose. Usually starting out as a tight bun, it would soon be streaming out behind in golden waves, her pretty face flushed and happy as she most always "won" the race.

The girls, though, contented themselves with animals of a different stature. A few years earlier Green had purchased a pair of fine riding ponies for the sisters. Now, the girls were allowed to ride their ponies to the one-room school they attended, but only as weather permitted. When the weather was raw or snowing, they would ride with their older brother Harry in the covered buggy.

Although big brother Harry was helpful in many ways to his younger sisters, he sometimes "went overboard" with his ideas of helpfulness. Once, the girls came home to tell their parents that their teacher, Mrs. Smith, had found "lice" in a student's hair. She wanted to make sure all of the students washed their hair thoroughly and treated their heads for lice before returning to school. Harry decided it was best just to shave the girls' hair, thus taking care of the problem permanently. As their parents were not at home, he held the girls down and shaved their heads, to loud cries and protests from both!

Understandably, Liz never quite forgave her brother for

his "helpfulness." She was so ashamed of her shaved head that she wore a bonnet for more than a month until her hair grew back. She had been very proud of her long golden-brown curls, and when it finally grew back it was a darker color and not so curly.

Little Lou was still crying when her parents got home. Green gave Harry a strong tongue lashing for taking matters into his own hands without waiting for consent from them.

In the fall of 1895 the weather was mild and the girls enjoyed riding their ponies through the fall leaves and down the country road to their school. The trees were red and yellow, golden and beautiful after the first frost. Chestnuts covered the ground in shady areas, and the girls often gathered them to take home. It was not unusual for them to see deer, wild turkeys, wild boar, and once in a while, a mother brown bear with her cubs.

The girls knew to stay clear of these animals, and would guide their ponies away from the danger. As long as the girls stayed on the old road to the school, they were fairly safe from predators even though there were cougars and large wild cats in the woods.

Harry had given Liz a rifle and taught her how to use it. He bragged to his buddies about how good a shot she was, and told them, "Better not mess with my sisters!" It was fortunate that Liz had learned how to use the gun, because one morning a large cougar tracked them. The ponies were spooked and reared up, tossing Liz and Lou to the ground. But Liz kept her head. Holding on to the gun, she quickly aimed and fired at the animal before it could charge. She must have hit it, because it yelped and ran off into the woods. The girls had to walk the rest of the way to school with Lou crying all the way. When they got there, the ponies were peacefully grazing, as if nothing had happened.

Their teacher and some of the older boys were preparing to go look for them when the girls arrived. The teacher had been worried when the ponies had showed up at school without the girls. When the girls related the story to the classmates, Liz was called a "heroine" for shooting the cougar. She did not feel brave, however. She felt very shaky inside and wanted only to go home where she could really feel safe. Lou kept crying for a long time and the teacher had a hard time comforting her. The next day, Green and several of the men went on a cougar hunt. They assured the little girls that that particular cougar would not bother them any longer.

Liz finished the eight grades at the top of her class, and went on to Normal College. She obtained a certificate to teach all grades from first to eighth. She became the teacher in the same small one room school where she and her brothers and sisters had attended as children.

The school had been repaired many times, adding a new roof, refurbishing the seats and blackboard, adding a few playground swings and a teeter-totter. Green and some of the neighbors had built most of this new equipment for the school and Liz was proud of her father's help.

Liz was still riding her horse to school, strapping the books and papers she would need to the saddle. She wore a "split" skirt, long tie-up boots, and always wore a bonnet or some sort of hat. Her skin was creamy and pink with a few freckles spread across her pretty little nose. She had a broad forehead and wide sky-blue eyes framed with long golden lashes and well-defined eyebrows. Her lips were full and red and she had a wide happy smile. And she smiled often. She was not tall, only about five feet, and weighed a mere 100 pounds.

But her grace and femininity was so obvious, that men stopped to stare when she passed by. The older boys in the school were so fond of her that they would gladly do anything she asked of them. In fact, they came early on cold mornings to build up the fire in the Franklin stove, and they tied up the horses that the children rode to school and saw that they were cared for during the day. The great black horse that Green had given Liz to ride to school was a fine animal, but stubborn and hard to manage. He had a "hard mouth" and often refused to obey Liz's commands.

Liz had complained about him to her father, who just shrugged. "Well, Sis," he said, "you just have to show him who's boss."

One early morning a storm was gathering in the West. Lightening and thunder could be heard, and as the storm grew nearer rain began to fall. Liz was anxious to get to school before the storm hit, and although she urged the horse on, the stubborn animal refused to go any further than a large yellow pine. There he obstinantly parked himself beneath the branches and no amount of coaxing or prodding could make the animal move. Grumbling, Liz finally climbed down and walked the remaining mile or so to the school with her school materials on her back.

A short time later, just as she was settling the children to their tasks, the storm hit. It was a fierce storm, and some of the smaller children were very frightened. Lightening and thunder crashed all around the small schoolhouse, and heavy rain pelted the roof. Liz gathered all the children to the front of the room, the older children holding the younger ones on their laps. She read them some funny stories, using the light of a large kerosene lantern.

After the classes were over that afternoon, two of the older girls walked with Liz to find her horse. They found him, dead beneath the pine tree! The tree had been hit by lightening, killing the horse where he stood.

Later that evening, Liz told her Pa it was probably about time for a more obedient mount. Green, noticing the rebuke in her voice, raised his eyebrows. "Well,' he replied, "I think we can find you an old mule, but mules can be stubborn too," he laughed.

Liz raised one eyebrow and said, "Huh! Like some men I know." Both Liz and her Pa laughed, although they were sorry to lose such a fine, though contrary, animal.

Not all of Liz's pupils were helpful and cooperative. One very large boy in the seventh grade was surly and bad mannered. He missed school so much that he was held in the seventh when he should have been doing eighth grade work. He used foul language and bullied the smaller children. Liz had threatened to expel him, but hoped she wouldn't have to carry out her threat, because she knew how much the boy needed to get as much education as was possible.

One day after a very difficult time with Oscar, Liz asked him to go home and not return until he could apologize to her and the other children. Oscar refused, and shouted that no one could make him do anything he didn't want to do. Liz motioned to two of the bigger boys to grab Oscar and hold him down across her desk. After a struggle in which several larger girls added their strength, Liz took a stout switch and gave Oscar's backside a sound thrashing. When the boys released him, Oscar ran crying from the school.

Liz called a recess to give everyone time to calm down before the afternoon classes began. Thrashing a student was not one of the things that happened very often, and for Liz, as a teacher, it was extremely rare. She found that she was quite upset and had difficulty concentrating the rest of the day. The episode was still on her mind as she rode home that evening.

The Grumpy Backpack

Have you ever seen a grumpy child?
And seldom see him smile?
He carries grumps in his backpack
And drags it all the while
He's very fussy with his food
Not liking this and that.
And when he's asked to play a game,
He always wants to bat!
He shoves himself into the line
And will not take his turn,
So in despair, his parents moan
And think he'll never learn!
And then one day our grumpy lad
Met a lovely little girl,
She looked at him and gave a smile,
And left him with a twirl!
"Please come back," said grumpy guy,
And said it with a grin,
So she came back and took his hand
And winked at him again.
"Leave that grumpy backpack here,
Just throw it in the Sea,
We'll travel down this lovely road
And happy we will be!"
It wasn't easy for our lad
To leave that pack behind
And see it floating out to Sea,
But soon he didn't mind
It's much more fun to laugh and sing
And in the fun to join
His shoulders felt so light and free
Without that backpack on!

She lived with her parents in a large farmhouse, about three miles from the school. It was growing dark, and the sun had already set. The long shadows of evening laced across the road. Her horse was skittish and several times Liz felt something was trailing her, although she did not see anything or anyone. She pulled her horse to a stop and sat quietly, listening. Nothing. The woods around her were unusually quiet, not a bird song, or the rustle of a branch.

It seemed to Liz that everything was too quiet. A chill ran down her spine, and she urged her horse into a gallop. When she reached the farm, she was out of breath and very frightened. Of what, she was not sure. But instinctively, she knew that she had, indeed, been followed. And, this time, it was not a cougar, but a two-legged creature…Oscar, she knew with certainty…he did not have any good intentions on his mind.

She called to her brother Harry, to come attend the horse, and ran into the house. She found her Pa reading in the living room, sitting before a large fire in the fireplace. He looked up at Liz and immediately knew that something was amiss. Liz quickly explained to her Pa all the happenings that day, including the ride home and the feeling that she was being followed.

"Do you think it was Oscar following you?" her Pa asked, laying the paper aside. Looking at her, the older man had a sudden feeling of fear for this little daughter, and a surge of protectiveness.

"Well," she answered, "I don't know for sure, but it was just a feeling, you know."

She pulled the bow from her long ponytail and shook out her golden mass of curls. She was rumpled and tired, and remembering when, as a child, the cougar had chased her and sister Lou. She shuddered, and sank down on the stool before the fire.

Her father leaned over and put his arms around her. "You're tired, honey. Go take a bath and you'll feel much better. We'll handle this Oscar business later."

Instantly feeling better, Liz kissed the top of her Pa's head and went off to fill the tub for a hot bath. Green, however, was feeling a sense of unease. He called to Harry, his oldest son, and together they circled the house and barns, looking for any sign of trouble or mischief.

"Look, Pa," Harry yelled. "There's someone messing around down near the store."

As the two ran toward the country store, located at the front of the property near the road, they saw two figures running off into the woods. Harry yelled for them to stop, but they disappeared into the underbrush. When Green and Harry reached the front of the store, they came upon their large German shepherd dog, lying motionless on the ground. He was unconscious, with a large bloody cut on his head. The smell of gasoline permiated the air, and they soon discovered a small bundle old rags, wet with gasoline, stuffed into a broken window.

Someone had tried to burn them out, and would have succeeded if they had not acted on Green's hunch. They gently lifted the dog and carried him to the house. Green sent Harry for the local vet. The dog, Buster, although badly cut and weak from loss of blood was already waking up and looking around.

"He'll be all right," the vet pronounced after a few minutes of examination. "Just needs rest and care for a few days."

Liz's parents, Green and Sarah Seagraves, owned and operated the only country store in that area of the county. They stocked everything from saddles to cooking wares, some groceries, milk, meat and vegetables. In one part of the large warehouse building, Sarah managed the yard goods. She sold materials for dresses, curtains, bedding and other necessities. It being a long trek to Huntington or Lexington, the nearest large cities, the store did well, and was popular with all the farmers who were happy to do their shopping near their homes.

Very few people had fire insurance in those days. Green knew that if the store had burned, he would have been ruined. He felt pain and anger in the pit of his stomach.

Who were those men and what did they have against him, he wondered? He understood the sinister nature of their intent. He set his jaw! He would not be intimidated. He would handle this in his own way. He told Sarah that he was going to sleep in the store for a few nights. Taking his rifle, their small terrier dog, a blanket and pillow he went down to the store and made he and the dog a bed in the front of the building.

On the third night, Green was awakened by the smell of gasoline, and the little terrier's barking. He grabbed the rifle and ran to the front door. He saw two figures running away from the store.

"Stop!" He called, and raised the rifle. "Stop or I'll shoot!"

The two figures kept running. Green took careful aim and pulled the trigger. The larger of the two men fell instantly to the ground. The smaller man paused for only a moment, and then dashed toward the trees where he disappeared into the darkness.

Green half carried, half dragged the heavy, inert man to the store. The injured man began moaning and twisting, trying to get away. Rolling him on his stomach, Green tied the man's hands behind his back, then dressed the wound as best he could.

"Hey, Sheriff," he said into the phone a few minutes later, "this is Green. I've got a two-legged polecat here. He tried to burn me out. He tried it once before, but this time he got a bullet in his backside for his trouble."

Green explained where they were, and informed the sheriff of the other "man" who ran off into the woods. Green recognized his prisoner as the good-for-nothing father of Oscar, the student that Liz had punished.

"Was that your boy with you?" Green asked.

"Yeah, that were me kid," the man mumbled. "That gal of yours had no call to whup my kid," and he spat on the floor to make his point.

"Well," said Green "You're setting a fine example for the kid. Sneaking around in the dark trying to destroy other people's property, doing the devil's work."

The Sheriff, Tom Sweeney, arrived and took the man into custody. Oscar was picked up a short time later as he was hiding under the porch at their rickety old share crop cabin. Both were taken to the County Seat.

The father was tried and sentenced to serve ten years for attempted arson. His sentence was to begin as soon as he recovered from the gunshot wound. Oscar was sent to reform school where he would stay until he was eighteen. The judge who sentenced them was lenient, considering it was not a first offense for either of them. The father and son had been in trouble many times in the past.

Surprisingly, for Oscar, reform school proved to be a good thing. He was forced to complete his schoolwork, and found that he enjoyed working on motors and engines. Once he got over his bravado behavior, he became a fairly well behaved inmate. His long skinny body filled out with muscles, and for the first time in his life, he had decent meals, adequate clothing, and a warm bed.

Oscar was paroled when he turned eighteen. He returned to his home a very different young man than when he left. His Pa was still in prison, and his Ma and two younger sisters were living hand-to-mouth, barely, just barely making it...Oscar persuaded his Ma and his sisters to leave the area and travel out West where he was sure he could get a job working on the "new-fangled automobiles." But before he left he had one visit to make. He found Liz alone as she was closing up the school for the night. Looking up, Liz did not recognize the nice looking young man as he walked between the seats to her desk.

"Can I help you?" she asked.

"Hullo, Miss Elizabeth, don't ye remember me? I'm Oscar." He smiled, a little hesitatingly.

"For goodness sakes, it is Oscar," she said, getting up and extending her hand. Oscar took her hand and shook it firmly. "I jest cum by to tell you, well to tell you I be leaving these parts soon, takin' me Ma and me sisters out West" He lowered his eyes, looking down at the floor. "Well, I jest wanted to say I'm real sorry fer being so rotten mean to you and I hope ye don't hold me no grudges."

Liz graciously accepted his apology, and said that she wished the very best for he and his family. She even got a promise from him to write to her and tell her how he was doing. She reached in her pocket and took out some bills about ten dollars (a great deal of money in those days) folded them and handed them to the young man. "This is a loan, Oscar, just to help you on your travels," she smiled. "You can pay me back when you are settled and have a job. " Oscar's face flushed, and he stammered that he didn't know "whut" to say. He tucked the money into a side pocket, and solemnly vowed to "pay back every cent."

Two years later Liz received a letter from Oscar. It contained the ten dollars and a note that he and his Ma and sisters were doing fine. They liked California, and all four had good jobs working for the Limonier Company, packing lemons and making lemon juice to sell all over the "whole country." He enclosed a snapshot of himself and his family standing under a palm tree with lemon groves in the background. They were living, he said, in a town called Montalvo. It was near the Pacific Ocean, and "right purty around here." He also wrote that he had met a "gal who is a real looker" and that they planned to get married. "Her Pa is the local preacher here, and said he'd marry us right in the church where me, Ma and the girls attend."

Liz held the letter, the money and the snapshot in her hand for a long time remembering the bad-mouthed boy she had thrashed with a switch those many years ago. A smile crossed her face, and her eyes filled with tears. She coughed and blew her nose. Sometimes, she thought, our prayers are answered and things do work out right. She tucked the letter away to show it to her parents.

During the summer months when school was out, Liz worked in her parent's country store. She relieved her Ma during canning season when Sarah "put up" the excess vegetables and fruit that they grew on the farm. Green and her two brothers Harry and Payton loved trains. The boys had prevailed on their father to buy a train set to put in the store at Christmas time. Harry had built a small village and Payton had made a tunnel and roads crossing the small tracks. The two would have played with the train set all day if their Pa hadn't objected. But on a farm there is much to do, and the boys knew they had to do their share.

The boys were not the only ones to enjoy the trains. One young man came in often to "play" with the trains, but he used it as an excuse to talk to Liz. He was tall, with a shock of black hair and piercing blue eyes. He had a broad smile that showed even white teeth. Liz had not failed to notice how good-looking he was, and had managed to learn that his name was Benjamin Ernest Young. She also learned that he worked for the railroad company, doing what, she was unable to find out.

Ben, as he was called by most of his friends, would come into the store regularly for a few weeks, and then would be gone for a long time, sometimes over a month or so. He never explained himself, and Liz did not ask, although she did miss him when he was gone. As the days grew shorter during the fall months she often worked for her Pa at the store during the evenings and on Saturdays. In the evenings after work, Liz walked up the long lane to her home. It was very dark, with trees and underbrush flanking each side of the lane. Old Marty, the negro man that Green hired to do extra work around the store, would walk behind Liz, keeping an eye on her until she reached her house. Liz appreciated his company, although he never walked close enough to her for the two to talk.

Green was especially grateful to Marty. He once tried to give him extra money, but Marty shook his head and said, "Wy no, Boss, it ain't no trouble fer me at all. I'se jest glad to do it fer Miz Liz."

Three weeks before Christmas, Ben came into the store. He smiled at Liz, and started to operate the little train set, making it travel along its little track and snake through the tunnel and over the bridges. Liz was waiting on a customer who was undecided about what color of material to buy for her little girls. Liz suggested red and white, Christmas colors. The countrywoman shook her head. No – she thought that would be "too flashy" for little girls. She finally decided on dark blue and bought pink ribbons for their hair. After the customer left, Ben walked to the counter where Liz was folding the material and arranging the shelves.

"Hi, beautiful" Ben said in a soft husky southern drawl. "How about if I walked you home tonight? It's getting right dark up that lane to your house."

Liz smiled at him; her heart was beating double time and she felt a tingle of excitement. She realized that she liked this handsome man. "I reckon it would be alright," she said. "Just wait a few minutes until I can finish up here, and tell Marty that he won't have to see me home tonight."

For the next two weeks, Ben and Liz saw each other every day. They went for long walks, sat on the railing of the bridge that crossed the creek and talked and talked. Even in the cold, as the winter wind whipped around them, they felt warm and alive. Ben found secluded places where they could be alone. His kisses excited Liz, and her lips were warm and inviting to Ben. He was asked to share Christmas dinner with her family who seemed to be genuinely fond of Ben.

In his heart, Ben was feeling that he wanted and needed this lovely young woman. He knew that he was in love with her, and wanted to marry her, but he realized that he could not marry, not now. He had dangerous work to do, and, he had a job to complete.

All through that Christmas day and into the evening as the family sang Christmas carols and opened gifts, Ben kept up a lively conversation. In the back of his mind, however, he was pondering just how he could approach the subject of marriage to Elizabeth. As he was a man who seldom "beat about the bush" he approached it head-on.

"Will you wait for me, Elizabeth?" he asked as they were walking home the next day after Liz finished work...

Liz looked up at him, and squeezed his hand. He had taken her mitten off and was holding her hand under his leather jacket. The snow was falling softly and the wind was cold.

"Yes, I'll wait for you, forever, but I hope it won't take that long." She snuggled close to Ben and felt the wild pounding of his heart.

Ben hugged her close and said, "I want you to marry me, Liz, but it can't be right away. You see, I have a job that will take me far away out West, and I won't be back for several months, maybe a year." He kissed her again and whispered, Are you sure darlin' that you want to wait that long?"

"Oh Ben, if you promise to take care of yourself, and write to me often, I guess I can wait. It'll be hard, but I'll make it." Her laugh was soft and musical.

Ben loved her so much; he didn't see how he would stand to be away from her. As it turned out he was gone for over a year and a half. He wrote her long letters, filled with his love for her, and often describing the work he was doing for a railroad detective agency. His work was strictly confidential, so Liz kept his letters to herself. She only read small parts of them to her parents, and kept the letters locked in her small cedar chest under her bed.

Finally a date was set for the wedding. Liz's older sister, Cora, who lived in a large two-story house in town, offered her home as a wedding chapel. Liz had written Ben about the offer and he said he was happy about it. "I'll arrive on the train, and bring the preacher with me," he wrote.

The date was set for Sept. 24th, 1912. Liz and Cora decorated the lovely home with flowers, bows, and ribbons. Liz wore a long gown of soft pale blue satin to match her lovely eyes. She tied part of her hair up into a crescent on top of her head, leaving strands of the golden curls to cascade down her back and over her shoulders.

The wedding dinner was prepared to be served at six o'clock: baked ham, whipped potatoes, green beans from the garden, ripe red tomatoes, and fresh leafy lettuce. There was roast beef and crispy fried chicken as well as pies and cookies and a beautifully decorated wedding cake.

The train was to arrive at 5 p.m. It did not arrive until nearly midnight! Ben had managed to call to tell the wedding party that there had been trouble with the track. The supper grew cold, the wedding guests were served, and most of them went home, Liz began to feel very tired and discouraged, however, the train did arrive, just before midnight.

The wedding took place as planned, even with a very tired bride and groom and a most bedraggled preacher. They ate a cold supper. There was much laughing and singing, as apple and berry wine was passed around the small wedding party.

"What's that?" Ben asked as he looked toward the front of the house. A loud ringing of bells and shouting was heard from the outside. "Oh no, not a shivoree,' Ben said, laughing.

He went to the door and walked out on the porch, the other guests and family following him. A large group of young people ringing bells and other noisemakers were shouting for the bride and groom to "come down." Ben walked over to a chair on the porch and picked up a large box. He took out cigars for all the men, and gaily wrapped candies for the women. The crowd was pleased with the gifts, and after a few more loud rounds of bell ringing, they broke up and wandered off to their homes, laughing and singing.

"I'm shore glad I came prepared," Ben said in his southern drawl.

"Yeah," answered Green, "sometimes, if the groom doesn't have treats, he gets carried off and has tricks played on him."

Henry, Cora's husband, laughed and said he remembered a fellow being "kidnapped" on his wedding day and put on the top of a barn, without a ladder.

"He was so mad he was purple! His hollering finally let someone know where he was," and Henry laughed heartily because he knew the groom, and enjoyed the joke played on him.

"Shivoree" or "belling" was a common practice in those parts. Many times, weddings were kept quiet, just to avoid these pranks. Cora and Henry wanted the newlyweds to remain overnight, but Ben had other plans. Even with Liz so tired, and Ben having had little sleep on the train, he was determined to take his new bride away. The preacher, however, was happy to accept Cora's hospitality.

Ben had a smart new covered rig with two great white horses waiting outside for them. He had arranged everything ahead of time. He helped Liz get her things together, shook hands with the wedding guests, expressed his gratitude for the use of Cora's home and the two of them climbed into the pretty little "buggy" and set off through the moonlight.

Elizabeth cuddled close to Ben, resting her head on his broad chest. She soon fell asleep, listening to the horse's hooves as they pulled the buggy and to the steady beating of Ben's heart. She didn't know how long or how far they traveled that night, but when Ben gently shook her awake, they were in front of a hotel in the city. Ben enfolded her in his arms and covered her mouth with kisses. They were lost in each other's arms for so long that the horses became agitated, wanting to be fed and watered.

As they pulled apart, Ben traced his finger down her jaw and across her swollen lips. “Come on” he said, “We have a whole lifetime to discover each other.”

Indeed, thus started a marriage that was to last for over 60 years. Ben and Elizabeth did become best friends, passionate lovers, excellent and caring parents and dedicated homemakers.

"Hoss" Young

CHAPTER THREE

A faithful man shall abound with blessings:

Proverbs: 29 : 20

Benjamin – 1886

BENJAMIN ERNEST Young was born near the small town of Henry, Virginia, in the summer of 1886. He was the youngest son in a family of seven children. Ben grew up on a large plantation, and attended a small one-room school through the 4th grade. He had been on his own since leaving the farm at 19, and shortly after the wedding he had decided to change jobs. A married man shouldn't keep the detective job, he felt, as it required him to travel so much, and was very often dangerous.

During the past year, he had tracked a man who was suspected of stealing a large sum of money from the railroad company. He followed his leads into Washington State to a logging and saw mill company. As his older brother Bill and his wife lived in this logging community, Ben went to their home to stay while he looked for the fugitive. The lumbermen there were big and burly, most with short tempers and all with suspicious natures.

Several weeks after Ben arrived at his brother's home, Ben spotted "his man" as he was lifting and hauling the heavy timbers to the sawmill. Alerting his brother, he told Bill he intended to confront the fugitive that next day.

The two approached the man trying not to cause suspicion but the man became instantly alert. Some instinct warned Ben that he was in great danger as these men had no trouble shooting first…then asking questions. Seeing the man reach for the pistol strapped to his side, Ben was quicker. He drew and fired, dropping the man in his tracks, a bullet through his right shoulder and his gun falling to the ground.

The man held his arm in pain as Ben walked to the man and stood over him, his gun still in his hand. "You're under arrest for the theft of that railroad payroll," he said, keeping his voice low and his pistol aimed at the man's head.

A group of workers had quickly crowded around, muttering and swearing, but none wished to challenge this lawman, and Ben was able to take the fugitive into custody without any further incident. Throughout the incident his brother Bill had stayed close, his gun drawn and ready, if necessary. Now, a year later, Ben did not wish to continue this dangerous occupation. Since the age of nineteen Ben had worked at whatever job he found. His father had died in an accident on the railroad when he was very young but the details of the accident had never been clear to the family. With his mother left alone with the large farm to run and no insurance, the only income was what the working farm could generate. As Ben was the youngest of the sons, his older brothers took over the running of the farm, and raising the cattle.

The Blacksmith Shop

(far left "Hoss", 2nd from the right "Payton")

But Ben was restless. He did not want to live on a farm, and he sold the acreage he'd inherited to his older brothers.

He had described the countryside around the small town of Henry, Virginia to Liz. By his description, Liz could picture the rolling hills covered with timber, the wildlife of bears, deer, wild cats, wild turkey and many other species of wild life. It was beautiful country, especially in the fall and spring of the year. The golden leaves of fall blanketed the forest trees with colors of red, orange, gold and the dark greens of the pines.

Ben loved the country in the fall of the year. The springtime was spectacular in its rebirth of new growth, mountain laurel, baby's breath, lilies, dogwood, and many other wild flowers. But Ben, feeling restless and wanting adventure was not happy and farm life was just too confining.

He loved his mother, sisters and brothers, and especially cared for his youngest sister, Bess, promising he would write to her and let the family know wherever his travels would take him. Bess had begged him to stay and work in the blacksmith shop with his brother Payton, and Ben had to admit he did like working there. But, he wanted to go out on his own and when he was nineteen he got a job with the railroad as a brakeman.

Ben loved to travel, and therefore liked the railroad, as it gave him an opportunity to travel and "see the world." The train stopped at small towns along his route, and Ben became acquainted with lots of folks in the small villages of Kentucky, West Virginia and Virginia.

Ben's big smile and happy demeanor won him instant friendships, and one of the friends he liked most was the owner of a mercantile store in a small town in West Virginia Will sold everything he could get his hands on, had a reputation of bartering, and was often in the midst of a great "bartering" operation when Ben rolled into town.

One afternoon, as Ben walked into the store, Will handed him a scrap of dirty paper. "Here, read this" he said. Ben took the paper and read, in very bad spelling and writing, the following note. "Stokpr, I hear ye all do sum tradin now and agin. Wull, I got sumpin to trade. Cum up to me place." The note was signed "Devil Eyes" and carried an added warning to "cum alone."

Will looked at Ben and said, "What do you suppose that old varmint has got to trade?" he asked, shaking his head.

"Well, I can't figure out, but I bet it's something you could use," Ben laughed, surveying the cluttered interior of the store.

The place smelled of tobacco, fish oil, varnish, musty books, old furniture and a mingling of spices. Bales of hay were piled to one side, along with chicken feed and a few live chickens in a coop near the back wall.

"I can tell ya one thing," Will uttered, blowing out a large, blue puff of cigar smoke, "I ain't a-gonna go up there by mu-self to thet hidey-hole!"

"Hell's fire, I'll go with you. I ain't scared of any of them polecats," said Ben, and he clapped his friend on the back, almost making him swallow his cigar.

Will coughed. "You mean it? You'll go with me?" His relief evident, Will knew he'd be safe with Ben as his friend had a reputation for taking care of himself.

The two men planned the trip up into the steep mountainous country. They tied rifles to their saddles, took extra grub and water and started off early the next morning. Ben wasn't quite sure where to find this hideout, however, he knew if he followed the trail upward, they'd find it.

Both men were extremely curious as to what the notorious Devil Eyes and his band of outlaws had to "trade."

As they rode their horses up the long winding trail into the mountains, Ben had an uneasy feeling at the pit of his stomach. He knew they were being watched, and trailed. Will, however, was unconscious of any such danger. He felt 'right safe" in Ben's company. He had great respect for this tall young man who was so capable of using his pistol, and seemingly afraid of nothing. Ben, on the other hand, had caught a glimpse of a rifle barrel sticking out of a bush beside the road and was on the alert.

As they rode along, the hair on the back of Ben's neck began to prickle. He kept his hand on the rifle butt and kept on riding up the trail. He didn't say a word to Will. Lord have mercy, he thought, that little guy is so easily spooked he might faint dead away on the trail!

Will was complaining about the long ride, the heat and his sore bottom when they rounded a bend in the road and saw one of the gang standing stock-still, pointing a rifle at them. Will yanked his horse so hard it reared up and almost upset him. Ben, who had been expecting something of this sort, pulled his horse up and sat perfectly still.

"You the stokeeper?" the man said as he eyed them both. Then, looking past Will he looked at Ben. "And who's this?" he asked, motioning with the rifle?

Will stammered. Then, remembering that the note said for him to come alone, he cleared his throat.

"This here is uh, Doc," he said weakly.

"Yeah? Whut kind o' Doc?"

"Oh, he's a hoss doc." Will answered, looking uneasily at Ben.

"Hoss doc, huh? Well we can use you, mister Hoss doc," he said, spitting a steaming stream of tobacco into the road. Without another word, he motioned the two men to dismount and follow him up the trail, leading their horses.

They walked for about a half-mile before coming to a well-hidden clearing in the thick forest. Ben looked around. There was a fairly good-sized old shack at one side of the clearing. Chickens and pigs rooted around the yard. A large mangy dog rose growling, and came toward them. "Naw!" said their escort to the dog, and the animal instantly dropped to the ground, still growling, but not moving . Will let out a sigh of relief. He was very happy to see such an obedient animal.

Ben was keeping his eye on his escort, and at the same time letting his eyes roam over the place. He felt uneasy, wondering just what "use" might be in store for him, since Will had chosen to call him a "Hoss doc." He would have to have a talk with that Will about his tall tales, especially when they involved him.

As all these things were going through Ben's mind, a tall, raw-boned old man stepped out of the shack and walked toward his "guests." He spit a stream of tobacco juice at their feet, and asked, as the other man had asked, "You be th' sto-keeper?" Then, pointing at Ben, asked "Who's this here?"

"Why, he's Hoss, the Hoss Doc," Will said warming up to his lie. "I brung him along just in case, ye know, just in case we had any trouble with, uh, the hosses."

"Humph," grunted the old man. "Wull, I'll have use fer ye later on. Rit now, we'uns are gonna see whut I got ye up here fer."

Ben had been aware of loud moans and barks that did not sound like dogs. The noise was coming from the back of a shed, behind the shack. Old Devil Eyes led them around to the back, where a large black bear was chained to a stout post, growling and moaning and straining at the chain. The old man stepped up close to the bear, making soothing sounds. Ben held his breath. The bear swung a giant paw and knocked the old man flat. Devil Eyes backed off, crawling like a crawdad on his back with the bear straining to reach him.

When he was clear, he got to his feet and wiped his bloody nose on a dirty sleeve. "He's gettin' too playful fer me, lately," the old man said, "I reckon I'll jest have to get rid o him." He shook his head as though he was very sorry to part with the animal. "That's whut I wanted you fer, sto-keeper," he continued. "I'll sell 'im to ye, fer meat, ye know, but ye'll need to take 'em down the trail before ye kill 'em. I jest couldn't do it meself."

He looked at the bear with real fondness. "Raised him frum a cub. Guess I got right mushy over 'im." His laugh sounded like a fingernail scraping tin.

Will became all business. He looked the bear over, from a distance of course, and studied just how much meat he would bring, how much trouble it would be to "take him down the trail" before he shot him, and what the horses would be like carrying the remains of a large bear back down the long trail.

He shook his head, "Noooo," he said, "can't see as how I can make any money on this critter. Nooo, jest can't do it."

And that was final. Will was in total control, and wouldn't change his mind; even after Devil Eyes offered him a big jug of "corn likker" as a bonus. The two men continued to "barter' for a while, but when it was obvious that the little storekeeper would not change his mind, the old man turned and latched his beady eyes on Ben.

Now, Ben had seen some mean looking fellers with meaner looks in their eyes, but he had never seen anyone exactly like this old man. Ben knew this man's reputation. It was said that he had personally shot over 20 men, and wounded as many more. Ben also knew that such tales were often exaggerated. Still, he was wary of this man and of "his boy, Josie" who stood off to one side, his rifle across his chest.

The old man turned to Ben, "So ye're a hoss doc, huh?" he drawled in his raspy voice. "Wull, come with me, I got a job fer ye."

His "boy" moved up to stand behind Ben, his rifle in a menacing position. Ben thought it wise to follow wherever he was taking him. During the "bartering" talk between Will and Devil Eyes, several of the old man's "boys" had appeared, seemingly from nowhere. They all stood around the two outsiders with less than friendly expressions on their faces. Devil Eyes led Ben around to a horse corral at the back of the clearing.

When Ben was ushered inside, he saw a young mare, lying on her side. She was covered with sweat and her breathing was labored and shallow. Ben realized that he had better try to act like the "hoss doc" that Will had told them he was. He stooped down and ran his hand along the side and stomach of the mare. Her whole body was swollen, but especially the abdomen.

"How long she been like this?" Ben asked.

"Wull, since yestiday, yestiday mornin'" said Devil Eyes. "She ain't about to foal I knows that, so whut the Sam hill is the matter with the fool thing?" He shook his head in disgust.

Josie stepped so close to Ben that Ben could smell his foul tobacco breath. "Effen ye know whut's good fer ye, ye sure better fix up this here mare. She be Pa's favorite." He pointed the gun at Ben's midsection.

"Stop pointing that damn gun at me!" and Ben grabbed the barrel of the rifle and pointed it to the ground. He was quick as lightening, and Josie was so surprised that the gun discharged, the bullet kicking up dust on the ground between the two men. The old man quickly stepped up between them and several of the other men had jumped forward. Ben had his pistol drawn, and was glaring at the assembled men. Will was so scared he was afraid he would wet his pants.

"Now, boys" growled the old man. "This feller is a doc, we be wise to let 'em git on with the doctoring."

The men stepped back, grumbling, and stood at a respectful distance as Ben again examined the mare. If she was not expecting a foal, he realized, her swollen belly could mean only one thing. She was swollen from eating poison weed, probably jimson weed, and if something weren't done soon, she would surely die.

Now Ben became "all business." He turned to the old man. "Fetch me hot water and rags," he said, "and some turpentine," he added, "and do it quick if you want this mare to live."

"Who ye ordering' around?" muttered Josie, still smarting from Ben's treatment. He stepped closer, but kept the gun pointed at the ground.

"Let the man do his job, Josie," the old man said. Miraculously, two buckets of hot water appeared along with several dirty rags and a tin of turpentine. Ben, having grown up on a farm, had seen cows in this shape from eating too green hay, or eating jimson weed, which could lead to the death of the animal.

Pulling off his shirt, Ben got down to business. He dipped the rags in the hot water then soaked them with turpentine. He started to rub the belly and sides of the mare with the hot treated rags. She didn't like it much, and rolled her eyes at Ben and feebly kicked at him. Ben kept at it, and Devil Eyes, realizing what Ben was doing, held the mare's head and made soothing sounds. After a few minutes, the mare gave a mighty belch,...then "belched" from the other end—several times.

Ben smiled. "Come on, you men; help me get her on her feet. And hold her up so she can't lie back down."

Several of the men jumped forward and lifted the mare to a standing position where continued to belch and fart for a few more minutes. Then, as if both horse and men were exhausted, the mare whinnied and trotted on her own over to the other side of the corral. A whoop went up from the men, and much backslapping took place. Seemingly, the "hoss doc" had been a real success!

As Ben put his shirt on, and washed his hands in the remaining bucket, he breathed a sigh of relief. He had a feeling that if the results of his "hoss doctoring" had gone the other way, well, he didn't want to think about it.

The men became right friendly as their visitors prepared to leave. Devil Eyes insisted on loading them down with jugs of "corn likker" and Will didn't object one bit. He figured he could sell the stuff for a good profit. That Will, thought Ben, always an eye for the buck.

When the two men were saddling up and preparing to leave the mountain hideout, Ben had turned to the old man and suggested he lead the bear far out in the woods and turn him loose.

"He'll probably be right difficult to "lead," but I 'spect ya'all can figger it out. You could give him some corn likker, just to mellow him out," Ben added, with a laugh.

The men laughed and talked about just who might get "the honor" of leading that "bar." Ben often wondered just what happened to the "bar," but his job with the railroad took him north so he never found out.

And, Ben would acquire a new nickname. As this story

would be told and re-told around the small towns near Will's store, for the rest of his life Ben would be known as "Hoss," especially in the railroad community,.

As he remembered these past episodes in his young life, Ben was surer than ever that he wanted to make the rest of his life with Liz, as safe as possible. After the "honeymoon" which consisted of a few days in the lovely old hotel in Ashland, Kentucky, Ben and Liz moved to West Virginia where he had found a job with a mining company.

Although he had only finished 4th grade in public school he had continued to study through correspondence courses and obtained certificates in Mining, Electrical and Diesel engineering. Now, being well qualified for most of the jobs open throughout the area, he had no trouble finding work.

But women see things differently. Liz felt his new job with the mining company was just as dangerous as the detective work, but kept quiet and did her best to adjust to this new life, so different from her former home and family.

Ben took the job of electrical inspector in the mines. He was required to descend into the mines and keep the electrical equipment in repair, and Liz soon learned what was common knowledge to all miner's wives; that the sound of the wailing loud "whistle" from the mine meant trouble... usually terrible trouble, sending dread through the hearts of all in the mining community. It meant either a cave-in or some other disaster.

Ben was fortunate that during the years he spent in the mining community he was never caught in a mine disaster. However, he was always right there to lend a helping hand when needed.

In 1914 the young couple were blessed with their first child. Little Margaret Frances came into the world as a happy healthy baby. Always called "Maggie," she was the joy of her Daddy and the love of her Mommy. Her Grandmother, Sarah, who came to be with Liz for the birth of the baby, naturally thought the little blue-eyed girl "the prettiest child" in the world.

When the baby was 6 months old, Ben and Liz made a short visit to Virginia to see Ben's family. The visit turned out to be a real family reunion, with all the brothers and sisters and their families present. They met at Bess and Len's home for a grand picnic. Liz and little Maggie enjoyed the large family and the fun of this reunion.

Bess and Len lived in a big two-story home. The rolling hills and green lawns were especially lovely that summer. Liz quickly made friends with the other women, and Ben was able to catch up with all the family news. Liz loved Ben's family and especially his mother. Ben had told his mother that Liz had a lovely singing voice, and soon several members of the family gathered around the old piano, where they sang songs popular at that time and also sang hymns especially for Ben's mother.

When they returned to the coalfields Ben and Liz quickly resumed the many tasks and duties of their young lives. The workload was heavy for Liz. The mining town offered little "conveniences," Liz washed large loads of laundry on a washboard in a galvanized tub and hung the clothes on a clothesline in the backyard. Lugging the baskets of clothes and the baby was tiring and weary work. Liz would place little Maggie on the grass, pull her skirts and petticoats out in front of her and place a heavy flat iron on the dress. In this way, the child was "anchored" and could not crawl into trouble.

In these small mining communities there was a real shortage of living quarters for the miners. Ben and Liz opened their home as a boarding house, and of course, this meant much more work for Liz.

At the end of each shift the miners would come home covered with coal soot, dirty and tired. And Hungry! Lordy, thought Liz, how they can eat! She cooked large meals of meat and potatoes, corn and beans, and made so many apple pies that she felt she could make them in her sleep.

Ben hired a Negro woman to help out, and Liz was grateful for her help. It freed her to spend a little more time with her baby. The men loved the little girl, and would pick her up and hold her, transferring the coal dust to the child's pretty dresses. Liz tried to be patient, and succeeded for the most part. Two years later, Liz was expecting their second child. The baby was due in early March or late February.

Early December had been an especially rainy, cold month. The work of keeping the house clean, cooking large meals, tending to the household and little Maggie, was taking its toll on Liz. She often did not get to bed before midnight, and was up at dawn. She and Beulah, her helper had decorated the house for the Holidays. Ben had brought in a tree, and she and Beulah had made ornaments of popcorn and candy to adorn it.

It had been raining steadily for almost a week and the front yard was a quagmire of mud. The men would slip through the mud, dragging it into the house. Sarah and Green were visiting from Kentucky, and while Sarah watched little Maggie, Liz and Beulah, with Green's help, dragged some heavy boards to the front to make a walkway from the road to the front porch where Liz had asked the men to leave their muddy boots before going inside.

The three struggled to get this walkway finished by evening. That night Liz went into labor. She began having strong contractions, and Ben rushed to get the "mine" doctor who worked all night with Liz. Toward morning, a tiny male child was born. He was not breathing, and the doctor wrapped him in a warm blanket and put him on the end of the bed. Liz's' mother, Sarah, was assisting the doctor.

As the doctor continued to work with Liz, Sarah picked up the small bundle, and as she did, she felt it move. A tiny cry came from the small blue lips. Sarah quickly cleaned out the baby's mouth rubbed him vigorously and placed the tiny naked infant headfirst down between her ample breasts. She held him there, rubbing his back and keeping him warm until the doctor was able to take charge. He examined the tiny child.

The infant was so small that he fit in the palm of the doctor's big hand. He looked like a tiny old man, wrinkled and now growing quite red as blood began to circulate throughout his frame.

"Is the baby alive?" asked Liz weakly. "Is it a boy or a girl?"

"It's a boy, honey," Ben said.

He had been there in the room the whole time and was almost, if not quite, as tired as the doctor and Liz. Sarah carried the baby, now wrapped warmly in blankets, to Liz, who moved so that the tiny mouth was near her breast. Wonders of all wonders, the baby began to suckle vigorously. Ben and the doctor both laughed, and the doctor sighed, relieved.

"You must be prepared, Ben," the doctor warned. "He is so tiny; I doubt he weighs more than a pound. You must be prepared to lose him. He probably won't make it." The doctor shook his head doubtfully. "I've never seen a child so small make it. He is almost two months premature, you know."

"Yes, I know." Ben said.

Regardless, Ben was determined to do all in his power to keep this tiny little son alive. He built a homemade incubator on the warm fireplace hearth. The baby was wrapped in soft warm blankets, and placed on his side when Liz was not holding him. Every day the doctor came, expecting the worst, but finding the tiny boy growing and doing quite well.

The little family, along with Sarah and Green and Beulah, enjoyed a great Christmas that year. The miners brought gifts for the baby and little Maggie. A group of Hungarian musicians gathered outside and played lovely Christmas carols. Nearly all the Hungarian men worked in the mines and spoke little English. However, they knew Ben and respected him.

Little Bartrum, nicknamed "Bart" also carried his father's name as a middle name. He was Bartrum Benjamin Young. "A lot of name for such a little squirt," Ben would laugh as he cuddled the baby. Little Bart thrived and grew.

He was walking by the time he was a year and a half old, and talking when he was two years old. His big sister Maggie adored him and made up endless games to play with her little brother. Bart was a stubborn child, and had a "mind of his own" about most things. He had bright blue eyes and an abundance of black hair, like his father. As he grew older his great passion was reading. His parents had a hard time keeping him in books. He would read and reread the same book many times and become lost in the world of the written page.

Ben was often impatient with the boy, and complained to Liz that Bart was a" dreamer" and might never amount to much. Ben, who had read only technical books all his life, had little patience with "nonsense" like fiction. Here, however, Liz was firm. She wanted her children to read, to like books, and to that end she saw to it that they had many fine works of literature. If she was unable to purchase the books, she took the children a library, even though it was almost a half-day's journey.

At night, after the chores were done, and the children washed and ready for bed, Liz would read to them from one of the classics. It was the favorite time of day for the family. Even Ben would sit and listen as Liz, with her lovely, expressive voice made the stories come alive.

The threat of war was in the air. Ben and Liz followed the news, and prayed that the President would, as he promised, keep the country out. Ben grumbled that he couldn't understand why the mess couldn't be cleared up.

"Why, they're all three of 'em cousins…and have the same grandmother, Queen Victoria, Why in tarnation can't they just sit down together and work things out?"

This Ben would say with a troubled expression, and Liz, with a sinking feeling, would agree, feeling there would be war, and that the U.S. would be pulled in.

And Liz's foreboding would once again be justified, as all too soon the country would indeed, be pulled into war. By 1918 more than a hundred thousand Americans would die—over ten million world-wide—and this Great War, this War to End All Wars would merely set the stage for an even greater conflict in the not too distant future, and that conflict would be responsible for the deaths of over fifty million.

The little family moved to Ashland, Kentucky, where Ben was offered a job as a diesel engineer at the American Rolling Mill Company (ARMCO). It was a good job, safer, thought Liz, than the mining work he had left behind. Ben was to continue working for ARMCO until his retirement when he reached the age of 65. He became a popular figure at the plant, where his nickname of "Hoss" followed him.

He and Liz bought a four-bedroom frame house on two

acres of land. They grew vegetables and raised chickens. Liz bought the milk and butter they needed from their next-door neighbors, and each year she bought a fresh side of smoked pork. Their neighbors, Mr. and Mrs. Cole had a large smokehouse, and raised pigs to sell. Liz complained about the "pig smell" but enjoyed the other smell (or rather aroma) of the pork as Mr. Cole was smoking it.

William Green, Liz and Ben's third child, was born in 1917, and twin boys had made their appearance into the family by the 1920's. Little Harry and Henry were blue-eyed blonds, with happy sunny natures. They were full of mischief and kept the whole family "hopping." Maggie and Will enjoyed these little brothers and had trouble telling them apart. Henry, who was much like his older brother, loved to read, and his favorite books were "westerns." When the twins would sit still long enough, Will would read to them.

At three years old, Harry, the more adventurous of the two, led his twin down to the garden. He had spotted some red "things" hanging on some plants. These red "things" were a magnet to him and he wanted to discover just what they were, and how they tasted. He wanted to taste everything. The little boys pulled two of the "red things" off the vine, smelled of them, and then each boy took a large bite.

"And then," Ben would laugh later, "all hell broke loose!"

The boys had their first taste of fiery red peppers! They screamed so loud that the entire neighborhood heard them. Liz and Maggie ran to see what was going on. Liz picked up Harry and Maggie carried Henry. They were taken inside where Liz washed their mouths with water, and gave them cool milk and bread. Liz and Maggie were laughing so hard they could hardly hold the boys still. Through his tears, Harry said indignantly that he shouldn't be "laughed at" when he was obviously going to die at any minute.

«Double Trouble»

When they were six, the boys accompanied their sister Maggie and big brothers to the Westfield Elementary School. They were bright students, and enjoyed school very much, although they continued their mischief making and were frequently a source of trouble to their teachers. They were mirror twins, and looked so much alike that Henry was often punished for something Harry had done. Neither boy ever "tattled" on the other, taking whatever punishment was handed out without too much complaining.

Liz had a rule that if one of her children were spanked at school, that child would be punished again when he or she got home. It didn't do any good to try to keep their Ma from learning about their mischief, Somehow she always knew and was waiting for them when they entered the house.

Bart, Will and the twins shared their father's love of machinery, cars and trains. Ben had purchased a large used Packard touring car. It was a beauty, rich black with spare tires on the front fenders and a canvas roof that folded back to make it open-air or "convertible." There were two fold-up seats on each side of the back seat and plenty of room for picnic baskets, sweaters and most anything the family wanted to take along.

The family loved to drive out into the country to Liz's sister Charlotte's home, where they had picnics and cook-outs on the large wide lawns. Ben had taught Bart how to drive, and although Bart was young, he was tall and large for his age, and could drive with skill. Most of the roads were graveled and narrow, but Bart handled the big car with little trouble. Liz complained that Bart drove "too fast," but Ben was confident of the boy's ability.

The summer months were happy times for the children, especially for the twins. There were apple trees to climb, wading and "fishing" in the creek that ran through the property, taking turns riding the new bicycle, and learning how to tie special knots for Cub Scout meetings. Maggie took the twins to Bible school during the first two weeks of June. At first they weren't' sure they wanted to go, but found it to be a lot of fun, with crafts, games and always good cookies and punch.

Both boys could never get enough cookies. They learned about David and Goliath, young Samuel, the Walls of Jericho, the feeding of the ten thousand, and many other Bible stories. At the end of each day's classes, the Pastor, Elder Rayborn would gather all the children and their teachers together and tell them stories. His stories were exciting and always had a good moral lesson that the children often didn't realize was a lesson. The stories made a big impression!

Summer passed into fall, with the rich colors of golds, yellows, and reds as the trees put on their finest "gowns." Liz and Maggie "put-up" jars and jars of green beans, stewed tomatoes, apple butter, peaches, sliced apples for making pies during the winter, and many kinds of vegetables, all grown in the kitchen garden.

The property surrounding the frame home was filled with apple trees. Some of the apples ripened in the spring and some in the fall. Will said that God must not like apples very well, because it seemed, that every summer one or two of the violent "thunder storms" with the fierce lightening would take out an apple tree. Ben would re-plant, but many of the trees were damaged and they had to be cut down.

Storms and floods were common along the Ohio valley and Westfield had its share. When the rains were heavy and frequent, the creeks swelled and overflowed, flooding the lowlands and ruining property and homes. The mighty Ohio River often flooded, causing much damage and loss of lives and property. Many years later, a floodwall was built that saved homes and also many lives from this sort of devastation. Ben and Liz had bought their home on top of a hill, and while they were never "flooded out," they were often left isolated by the floodwaters.

The twins would always remember the time Maggie had taken them to a spot on a hill nearby where they could see the extent of the flood waters, before the river had "crested." They saw tops of homes sticking out of the muddy waters as it swirled around, carrying off furniture, pigs, chickens, cows and sometimes people, clinging to logs, wooden chairs or loose boards. As the young people watched, a house came floating by with a man and woman and a dog clinging to the roof. It was something that stayed in the boys' minds for the rest of their lives. When the twins reached adulthood, they campaigned for the floodwall and had much influence in getting it built.

TO CATCH A BUTTERFLY

I'd like to catch a butterfly,
And fly up to the moon
I'd like to ride a dolphin's back
And not return 'till noon!
I'd like to eat an ice cream cone
And drip it down my chin
And jump my rope and count to ten
And always, always, Win!
I'd like to hear the blue bird's song
And catch it in a cup
And then, before I go to bed,
I'd drink that song right up!
I'd like to reach and catch a Star
And hold it in my hand
And when the soldiers came marching by
I'd put it in the band.
I'd like to walk into the woods
And find a big brown bear
I'd give him gum and chocolate bars
And then I'd comb his hair!
I'd like to catch a butterfly
And to the clouds we'd fly
And see an Angel floating near
She'd give us apple pie!

CHAPTER FOUR

Becka – 1923

THE WIND whipped around the small frame house, tearing at the roof and trying to get inside through closed doors and windows. Snow, mixed with sleet and rain pelted the house, and tree limbs whipped against the outer walls. It was a raw February night.

The folks inside the house were unaware of the weather; they were occupied with more important things. Young Maggie ran up and down the long center hall, carrying warm water and towels, and anything else the doctor had asked for. Ben hovered nearby, holding Liz's hand, and trying to be useful, but mostly getting in the way.

"Come-on Elizabeth," Ben urged, "let's get you up and walking for a while. Come on now, you can do it." And the doctor helped Ben lift Elizabeth to her feet. She moaned a little, but got up and began to walk up and down the long hall. The twins were already in bed, and Bart and Will had gone to spend the night with a friend. Ben had taken the night off from work so that he could be home. Liz walked

"Daddy's little girl"

laboriously up and down the central hall.

Her slippered feet straddled out, making Liz look like a giant duck, her body heavy and awkward. Ben walked with her, teasing her about the way she walked and looked causing her to give him a hard pinch.

"Sweetheart," Ben said, leaning close, "you've never looked lovelier to me than you do right now."

She raised her head to kiss him just as a very strong contraction hit. "Ooooohhhh," she groaned, "get me to the bedroom, quick!"

The baby was so impatient to make its appearance into this cold and rainy world, that it was born before Liz could remove her slippers! In a few minutes, after the doctor had performed the necessary care for mother and baby, the tiny, little girl was placed in her mother's arms. Ben leaned over the bed and kissed his very tired wife. Then he pulled the small pink blanket back so he could see the baby. She is so perfect, he thought. She had lots of black hair, and blue eyes.

"Well, Ben," said Liz, we have another little girl, just as you wanted. And she is my Valentine. Today is February 14th. We'll call her Rebecca Lou Valentine."

Even the storm outside, the war clouds gathering over Europe, and the political battles in Washington did not matter to those inside the small frame house this night. They were happy, and Elizabeth had her "Valentine."

Little Becka, as she was called, was healthy and grew quickly. She sat up when she was four months old, began to walk at nine months, and could talk by the time she was a year old. She often seemed to "study" the faces of her parents, her sister and her brothers. Many times, she could anticipate what others were going to do or say, and seemed to know ahead of time about events, before they happened.

Her oldest brother Bart took a great interest in this "funny little sister." He loved to carry her around, play games with her and, best of all, read to her.

Becka loved it and she adored Bart and Elizabeth was grateful for Bart's help with the baby. She had a house full of work, five other children in the family to cook for, chickens to feed, and large loads of washing, ironing, and mending that never seemed to end.

And Liz was grateful for the help she received. Beulah came to help two or three times a week. She had moved to Ashland at the same time Elizabeth and Ben had moved from the coalfields of West Virginia. She had married a widowed Negro man from the country, and they settled in a small place on a nearby farm where her husband worked. She had no children, and both she and her husband, who was much older, did not want to start a family.

Things were not easy for Negro families in those days. Schools were segregated, and although the Negro was "free," there were a lot of things that were off limits to them. Happy to work for Elizabeth, Beulah came to love the children as her own. In Ben and Liz's home she was treated as though she were family, having authority to discipline the children.

And the children respected her authority. She was always fair, but firm, and when there was mischief – and there often was – it was Beulah rather than Liz who used the switch. And to great effect. The twins learned to behave themselves when Beulah was around. With Bart's help she had learned to read and write. Learning to read had always been a dream of Beulah's.

Elizabeth made clothes for herself and her children, and often made dresses and shirts for Beulah and her husband. Eggs and bacon, vegetables and meat went home with

Beulah on a regular basis. Beulah remembered the "coal field" days and the birth of Bart. She remembered how she and Elizabeth had carried the heavy boards to the front yard of the boarding house, and the difficult times with the mud, rain, dirty miners, the endless cooking and cleaning.

She felt that the work here in Kentucky was not nearly so hard, and she was so happy to be with this family again. Beulah was an honest, hard-working woman. She was a "born again" Christian, and practiced her beliefs.

One summer when Becka was two years old, Beulah took all six of the youngsters with her to a "revival meeting." The meeting was being held in a large tent in a nearby field. Little Becka sat on Beulah's lap and clapped her little hands to the wonderful "soul" music. There was much singing, shouting, and dancing. Folks were making their "confessions" and asking to be baptized.

The baptisms were to take place the following Sunday in a nearby creek. All the children begged Elizabeth to let them go with Beulah to see this "wondrous thing" and Elizabeth consented. The children were quiet and respectful as each candidate for baptism was led down into the water. As each "sinner" was plunged beneath the waters of the creek, a loud chant rose up, with much shouting, singing and clapping. It was altogether a very happy affair, and the children would remember that day with a feeling of joy.

Beulah had great affection for all six of the children. However, her favorites were Bart and Becka. Bart had been very helpful to Beulah, teaching her to read and to write. He showed her how to keep track of her family accounts, and often read the paper to her, keeping her aware of what was happening in the world beyond the small community in which she lived.

Bart found that Beulah was intelligent, and learned quickly. She didn't feel "shamed" to let a teenage boy be her teacher. She was proud of Bart and found him to be a patient and thorough instructor. Even as she learned to read and write, she never completely altered her way of talking to the speech of "white folks" but retained her dialect unchanged.

Elizabeth did not object to Bart's helping Beulah with "schooling;" she thought it was a good thing for them both. Beulah never neglected her work, so Ben voiced no objections either. As Beulah learned, she held Becka on her lap, and little Becka, although only two years old learned also. By the time she was three and a half Becka was reading and printing her name. She was also reading almost anything, although not always with comprehension.

It was at about this age that Becka began having her "vivid dreams." Feeling she was getting too much stimulation from all of the reading with Bart and Beulah, her parents decided perhaps she should play with the younger children.

"She is growing up much too fast," Ben would often remark.

However, there were no younger children with whom the youngster could play. There were no close neighbors with small children, and the twins were occupied with the rough and tumble world of young active boys.

As Becka grew a little older, Harry started to play with her more often. He found that she loved to climb trees as much as he did. The two often climbed to the top of the largest apple tree and played games of "Tarzan of the Apes" or "Space Man."

The games were mostly of Harry's imagination, but Becka had some good ideas of her own. She loved to play with her dolls, and often Harry would include a doll in the make-believe.

Sometimes Henry joined in the games of imagination, but it was Harry and Becka who were the "leaders." Henry did not seem to mind just being a follower. He was often occupied with other activities and Harry and Becka were alone in their world of "make-believe."

Becka wore overalls and begged her mother to cut her hair like Harry's was cut. She was often involved in the rough and tumble world of little boys . One afternoon Ben was looking out the window as he sat at his library table. He was amused to see two little boys tumbling around, and scuffling. Then he realized that one of the little "boys" was a girl, and it was Becka! He got up and went outside, and taking Becka by the hand, he marched her into the kitchen where Liz was preparing dinner.

"Ma," he said in his southern drawl, "is this a girl or a boy?"

Liz smiled and looked at Becka. "Well," she answered, "it looks a little like a boy, doesn't it?" and she laughed.

"Well, Ma, let's put this child in a dress, and let her hair grow, so we can tell the difference!" With that, Ben tousled Becka's hair and walked back to his library table and his reading.

And from that day on, to Becka's dismay, she was not allowed to dress in overalls, go barefoot, or have her hair cut in a boy's bob. However, she still climbed trees with Harry and continued to play the wonderful games of imagination with her brothers.

One day, while teetering in the top of the apple tree, the two "Indian Scouts" watched as two elderly women came slowly down the road. They were pulling an old rusty wagon with wobbling wheels. The wagon was filled with day-old bread, rolls, scruffy looking vegetables, and various other edibles.

"I wonder where they get that stuff?" Becka asked Harry.

"Oh" he answered, "I think I heard Ma say that the store gives them the leftover stuff. They are very poor, you know, and there isn't a man, I mean a husband or a brother living with them to work and help with stuff. You know," he continued, "they live in that old farm house 'way over yonder on the hill."

"Oh," said Becka, her little heart filling with pity for the two old ladies.

"Ma and Pa tried to help them several times," Harry went on, "but they are such ornery old gals they chase everyone off who tries to help them."

Becka considered this as she watched the slow progress of the old women. She was so intent that she lost her hold on the tree branch and would have fallen out of the tree if Harry hadn't caught her.

The old woman named Lena looked up and saw the children. "I see you two brats up there," she said in a raspy voice. "I know who you are. Up to no good, that's what you are. If I had a good switch I'd warm your britches for you."

"Yeah, Yeah," yelled Harry "you'd have to catch us first. You're just a couple of old witches. Go back to your 'witches cave,' and Harry pulled an apple from the tree and threw it at Lena. It landed at her feet. She picked it up and put it in the wagon.

"Want some more?" Harry said, and began throwing apples into the road. Lena reached out her hands and caught the apples as the boy threw them. Handing the apples to Coonie, her sister would put them in the wagon. Very soon all four were laughing. When all the apples the children could reach were gone, Lena and Coonie looked up. With crooked toothless smiles, the old women waved, and pulled the wagon on down the road.

"Wow" said Harry to Becka. "What do you think of that?"

"I guess they're hungry and needed the apples. I'm glad we threw them out there." Becka's little face was sober as she added. "If I tell you something, will you keep it a secret, just between you and me?"

"Yes, Becka, you know I won't ever tell anything you don't want me to tell. Your secrets are my secrets," Harry said with assurance.

"Well, I had a dream about those old women, a very strange dream. I've never been in their house, but in my dream I saw the inside of the house. The bedroom where they sleep, and the kitchen, and the steps that lead to the upstairs and the rooms up there."

As Harry listened, Becka continued, "In the dream it was very cold. There was snow falling outside and the wind was blowing against the windows. Lena and Coonie were huddled together on a small bed. They were freezing cold. There wasn't any fire in the stove, and no food on the table or in the cupboard."

Becka looked at Harry. "Do you think I should tell Mama about the dream? It's summer time now. I don't know why I dreamed about it snowing."

"Well," answered Harry, "maybe you should tell Beulah first. Then if she thinks you ought to tell Ma, then I guess you ought to."

As they climbed down from the tree, Liz called from the porch that supper was ready. "Come in, and get your hands and faces washed,"

Becka washed her hands and face, all the while pondering what Harry had said. She made up her mind to take his advice, and confide in Beulah first. Becka felt that Beulah was a wise and helpful member of the family. She was too young to reason this out consciously, but knew instinctively Beulah would help her do what was right.

After supper was over, Maggie and Liz started cleaning up the kitchen. Beulah drew water for Becka's bath, and as she was helping the little girl get ready for bed, Becka told Beulah of the dream. Beulah listened without interruption as Becka related the dream.

"Do you think I should tell Mama?" Becka asked, looking at Beulah with wide questioning eyes.

"Yes, honey, I think you should tell your Mama. She'll know if the dream means something and what should be done about the pore old misses. I feel right sorry for them pore old misses," Beulah continued, "that I do. They be so contrary, they don't want no help." She shook her head, sadly. "So, I reckons they ain't much a body can do for 'em."

Before Becka was tucked into bed that night, she related her dream to Elizabeth. Months later, when the weather had turned cold and winter was approaching, Lena was to find freshly cut firewood, along with canned foods, outside her kitchen door. Firewood and food would appear two or three times a week, and Lena would smile her toothless smile and waved toward the house with the apple trees.

That summer, Liz called Becka in from playing. "I've got something to show you," she said, as Becka ran inside to see what her mother had for her. Liz handed Becka a long slender white box. When Becka opened it and pulled back the tissue paper, she found a beautiful doll. The doll had dark curly hair, sleeping eyes, and delicately painted features. She had a porcelain head, arms and legs, with a soft body. When she was turned over on her stomach, the doll cried "Ma Ma."

"Oh," cried Becka in delight "is she for me? She is so beautiful, Mama. I love her!"

"Yes" said Liz, "she is a present for you from your Aunt Cora. The doll belonged to your cousin Tay. She is a grown up woman now, and needs someone to take care of this dolly. Tay thought you might like to be the doll's new mama." And Liz put the doll into Becka's waiting arms. "I promise I'll take good care of her, Mama. She'll sleep with me every night, and I'll brush her hair, and keep her clean. Can I name her Tay?"

"Of course, honey," Liz answered. "You can name her Tay and I know you will take good care of her."

Liz tightly hugged both daughter and doll, silently hoping this new doll would somehow keep Becka from having those terrible dreams.

The doll went everywhere with Becka. She sat at the dinner table and "tasted" Becka's food, "sipping" her milk and nodding her head and crying "Ma Ma" with approval. The doll and the little girl added a touch of amusement and merriment to the dinner table. Soon the rest of the family treated Tay as a member of the family.

When Christmas arrived, Becka found matching dresses for herself and Tay under the tree. Will bought Becka a tiny little washing machine. It had a hand crank that pushed a little plunger up and down in the soapy water, so that Becka could wash Tay's clothes. That year, the Christmas following the summer when Becka received the doll was very mild. It was cold, but unfortunately, no snow fell for a "white" Christmas.

"How is Santa going to get here if there is no snow?" Becka asked her brother Bart.

"Don't worry," Bart told her. "He will come in his autogyro." Bart continued, "He'll land on the roof and come in through the kitchen door."

"Let me see! Let me see!" cried Becka.

"No, no, you have to stay inside or he won't stop at our house." Bart said. As if on cue, the loud sound of a motor was heard from outside. "Listen," Bart continued, raising his eyebrows, "I hear the sound of an autogyro now."

Becka had heard that sound before. It sounded to her like an electric motor her Daddy had out in the tool shed. But she didn't say so.

"Oh look," cried the twins, "here comes Santa Claus now!!"

A very large man came into the room. He was, dressed in a suit of long red underwear with white fur sown on the sleeves, the neck and the trousers; He had a white "beard," tall black boots, and cried "Ho! Ho! Ho!"as he swung the large red bag off his shoulders. He went to each stocking that was hung by the fireplace, and put candy and nuts in each one, then added oranges and bananas to fill them to the top. This was indeed a special treat as the only time the children had oranges or bananas was at Christmas time.

Santa then pulled a small red sled out of the bag and gave it to Becka. "Don't worry," he said, "It will surely snow before your birthday! Ho! Ho! Ho! I must be on my way. Lots of other good little children are waiting for me!" He turned and left the house, Ho, Ho, Hoing as he went.

Liz, the twins, Bart, Will and Becka were all laughing and clapping their hands. "Santa" had been a real surprise, at least to Becka. She had recognized Santa as her Daddy immediately, and went along with the performance as though she believed Santa was real. To Becka it was another good game of imagination. In the many years to come, she would to remember that she had never loved her Pa as much as she did that cold, very special Christmas morning.

And the snow did fall before her birthday, in abundance. Several times before Becka's birthday in February she and the twins would have much fun with the little red sled. Their old neighbors, Lena and Coonie allowed the children to use her hillside to slide down, stopping only when they reached the rock wall, where they would turn aside and go sliding up the lane.

Bart had secured a part-time job that spring, and purchased a motorcycle with the extra money. Liz was not happy about it, but said nothing, except to admonish Bart to "be very careful."

That summer, Becka had a dreadful, prophetic dream about Bart. In her dream she saw his motorcycle lying on the road, with Bart's crumpled body lying nearby. She awoke from the dream screaming, and begged Bart not to ride that day. But he had only smiled down at her with that special look and told her not to worry, and went roaring away down the street. Tears filled the young girls eyes as she watched his receeding figure.

During the weeks following the funeral, Beulah came to help the family in any way she could. She was as crushed by Bart's death as the rest of the family, loving this special young man as though he were her own son. One of the ways that Beulah helped was to give Becka special attention. She would take the little girl, along with her doll, Tay, and sit on the porch swing pushing the swing to and fro while talking quietly to the sobbing child.

"You mustn't be so sad, chile," she would say, "your brother, he's in Heaven now. He's with God, and he's happy there." Knowing of the girls dream she would hug the little girl tightly. "Don't you go blaming yourself about that dream, honey, you got a 'gift'....a gift from God. It ain't your fault Bart didn't listen. It's a true gift you have, chile. Someday you'll see." Most days she would kiss Becka, giving her the corner of her apron to blow her nose.

"But why did God have to take him?" Becka would sob.

"I don't want God to have him. I need him here with me. Why, why did God take him away when we all need him so much? Why?" and she would start to cry all over again.

"It is alright for you to cry, little honey," Beulah would say, soothingly. "You haven't really lost Bart. He's nearby. You just can't see him now. The veil is mighty thin betwixt you and Bart. Why, if'n you try, you can see him in your dreams. He'll come to you, and you will feel him near you. You just shut your little eyes, chile," she continued in her soft southern dialect, holding Becka close, "and think of him, and he'll be right there, you'll see. Just shut your little eyes and go to sleep right here on old Aunt Beulah's shoulder."

And Beulah cuddled Becka and her dolly close as Becka hiccupped and finally fell asleep. Becka remembered what Beulah had told her, and while she did not know if it were true or not, Bart did "come to her" in her dreams. She saw his smiling face, and felt his presence. When she awakened she felt better and almost happy again. The death of the oldest son was traumatic, not only for the parents but for the brothers, and Maggie as well. It would take a long time for the family to adjust to the loss.

That long summer, Liz and Ben planned many trips out to the country to visit Aunt Charlotte. It was good for the younger children and Maggie loved to visit with her older cousins, Charles and Frank, Jr. Becka and her brothers rode the horses, played in the creek, threw the ball for the great collie dog, and ate picnics on the wide green lawns. One long weekend Ben and Liz took all the children for a trip to Virginia Beach.

It was the first time that the twins and Becka had ever seen the Atlantic Ocean. It would have been a wonderful vacation except for the shrimp dinner Ben had ordered at a small restaurant near the beach. Becka and the twins had ordered shrimp also, but did not like it, so Ben had eaten his dinner and then finished off what the children had not eaten. Within an hour of the dinner, Ben had become violently ill. The shrimp was spoiled, and had given him a monumental bellyache! He was so sick that Will had to drive them all home, even though he was very young, and had no driver's license! Liz had never learned to drive. And Maggie did not know how to drive either. The twins and Becka were feeling sick also, and the family had to make many stops on the way back home. Yes, thought Liz afterwards, it was a long, long weekend! Liz also determined to learn to drive an automobile, if she could ever get the courage!!

Shortly after they arrived back home, she said to Ben as he sat reading on the front porch, "Ben, I want to learn to drive the car."

Ben looked at her and laughed, "You don't need to learn to drive, you have two men in the family to do the driving."

Liz looked at him for a moment longer, then turned and walked out to the back where the car was parked. "Come here, Will," she said with authority, "show me how to start this car!"

Will hesitated only a moment, then climbed into the car, turned the key and started the engine. Liz motioned for him to get out. When he climbed out Liz got in and looked at the pedals.

Humm, she thought, which one do I push to go forward. She knew where the gas pedal was, but didn't know just how to use the gearshift? Maggie had been watching her mother and gathered the children onto the back porch, looking worried. She debated if she should go get her father. She decided that she wouldn't. She, too, wanted to learn to drive, but her Pa had refused to teach her.

Liz pushed one of the gears forward and the car shot backward hitting the tool shed and pushing it off its foundation! One of the back wheels caught inside a large galvanized washtub, and the tub rotated with the wheel, making a "godawful" sound! Liz didn't know how to stop the car, and being afraid, Maggie wouldn't let Will go to help.

Ben heard the commotion and came outside to see what was going on. He quickly assessed the situation, ran and pulled the key out of the ignition. Then he began to laugh. All the children started to laugh also.

But not Liz! Humiliated and angry, she climbed out of the car, slammed into the house and went into the bedroom, slamming the door behind her.

Ben examined the car, and with Will's help managed to free the wheel from the washtub. It took some doing to get the tool shed back on its foundation. They had to pull it using a stout chain hooked to the rear of the Packard. The incident was never mentioned again, at least not in Liz's presence.

"Maggie Frances and Johnny"

CHAPTER FIVE

Maggie
The Depression Years
1930–1936

MAGGIE WAS developing into a mature, lovely young woman. She had fine curly brown hair, blue eyes, a broad forehead and the rounded curves of young womanhood. She had graduated from high school that spring and planned to attend college with the desire to become a teacher.

She was popular in school and had many "boy friends." Johnny, one of her new friends, called her often. However, Ben did not much care for this particular young man and did not want Maggie to go out with him. Of course, Ben's objections just made Maggie want to see Johnny more often.

"Why does Daddy not like Johnny?" Becka asked Harry as the two were playing in the yard.

"Well," answered Harry, "I heard Pa say he was a womanizer…whatever that means."

Becka pondered this answer. "Maybe it means he eyes women," Becka thought for a moment. "Or maybe it means that he hugs and kisses a lot, like he does to Maggie." She laughed.

"Oh, they do a lot of smooching?" Harry asked. He was picturing his big sister, with Johnny, "smooching it up." He thought of his well-developed sister, her golden brown hair and her full red lips. Oh yeah, he thought, Johnny would really enjoy "womanizing" Maggie. He did not voice his thoughts to Becka, however.

There were many crying screams and loud protests from Maggie, until Ben finally gave in and allowed Maggie and Johnny to go for walks together, but only if they took little Becka with them. And, Becka didn't realize, of course, that she was a sort of "chaperone" for the young couple.

At first, Becka thought these walks were a lot of fun. The young couple walked slowly, letting Becka set the pace. They walked through the park and over the footbridge that spanned a swift moving creek. They often took cookies and other goodies and sat on park benches to eat.

One Saturday afternoon as the three walked over the footbridge, Becka begged Maggie to let her play in the creek. Maggie saw no harm in it, and thinking this would keep her little sister occupied, consented. Maggie carefully removed the little girl's dress, shoes and socks and allowed her to wade in the shallow water. Becka was wearing only her underpants. Meanwhile the young couple climbed the grassy bank. There, sitting beneath a tree with overhanging branches they could keep an eye on Becka, but could not be seen from the bridge or footpath.

There was a lot of hugging and kissing going on, but

Becka was unconcerned with what her big sister and Johnny were doing. She was lost in a world of her own. She found muddy holes and nice squishy mud for her feet. She watched tiny minnows as they darted about beneath the water. She even saw a garden snake sunning himself on a rock across the creek. A very large crawdad was observing Becka's progress through the shallow water. When she got too close to him, he grabbed her big toe with his large pincers and hung on!

The girl's screams could be heard for a half-mile! Maggie and John were so startled by the screaming they almost rolled down the bank into the creek. Maggie jumped to her feet and ran toward Becka, forgetting she had on her best shoes. When she reached Becka, the child was screaming and staring at the large "monster" clinging to her big toe. Maggie took one look, and not about to touch that thing, yelled for Johnny.

"My God!" exclaimed Johnny, "What is all this fuss about?" He reached down, and grabbing the "monster" right behind its pincers, squeezed hard.

Relinquishing its hold on the toe, Johnny threw the offending creature into the deepest part of the creek and sat down on the bank, holding his sides with laughter. Becka, meanwhile, had scooted up the side of the bank and was now putting her toe in her mouth.

"Don't do that," Maggie said," Your feet are dirty and muddy!!" She tried to pull Becka's toe out of her mouth, but Becka shook her head and continued to suck on the injured toe.

Maggie decided this little episode should be kept between the three of them, knowing that surely her parents would not understand. And Becka agreed. She had a feeling that her Mama would be very unhappy with her for playing in the creek wearing only her underpants. "You know better, young lady", she could just hear her mother say, "you're getting too big for that sort of thing."

Yes, she thought, it would be much better to keep these things to ourselves. As the girl was getting dressed, the girls agreed that the episode of "the creek and the crawdad" should remain their special secret.

They left nodding in full agreement, prolonging their walk until all the clothes were dry. Maggie was not sure just how she would explain ruining her best shoes, but, "oh well," she thought, she'd come up with something.

Upon reaching home, they found their mother occupied in the kitchen. Greatful for this turn of fate, the girls were able to slip in and get cleaned up before Liz saw them. Becka could always confide in Harry, and knew he would never "tattle" on her. She related the story of the creek and the crawdad to Harry the next time they were alone. Harry laughed almost as hard as Johnny had laughed.

"Why are you laughing?" said Becka, feeling peeved.

Harry laughed again. "I'm just picturing you, sitting on the bank of that creek, in your bloomers, yelling your head off while a big ole crawdad chomps on your toe!"

This time Becka laughed with him realizing it actually was pretty funny. "Well," she said, after a moment, "I'm sure glad Johnny was there to get it off. Maggie sure wouldn't touch it." And at that the children laughed again.

Harry and Henry remained close, seldom having any disagreements, although they were beginning to have separate interests. Their taste in girls, however, remained the same. Sometimes when they 'had eyes' for the same girl, they settled it with a toss of a coin.

Having a gift for music, Harry started to play the violin when he was about eight years old. The school orchestra instructor encouraged him and provided a school violin for him to use. Henry wanted Harry to play in the orchestra also, but Harry preferred the piano and the guitar. As a "drummer" for the school band and enjoying it immensely, he wanted Henry to march in the band with him. So, he prevailed on his twin to "play the cymbals." This way both boys went to all the baseball games, football games and had a grand time in parades throughout much of high school. This would com to an end as Henry, enjoying sports much more than Harry, played football during his junior and senior years.

Maggie, seen as having the most musical talent in the family, was happy that the twins loved music. She encouraged them and helped them in their music lessons. Liz taught both girls to play piano Becka, had a fine voice for singing. During this period families often gathered around the piano making their own intertainment. Henry with his violin, Harry on the guitar, Maggie playing the piano, and Becka singing with Will joining in, the family would rarely get together before, at some point in the evening, a "music fest" would take place.

Elizabeth and Ben encouraged the artistic abilities of the children. Harry loved to draw, making pictures of all the family. He would take his pad and pencils and sketch the various things he saw around the small farm. The barn, the hay wagon, the chickens, the apple trees, the car that Pa drove to work; all were transformed on his easel. Harry made pencil drawings of his family with amazing results, and usually won any art contest he entered.

Liz could play the piano and had encouraged both Maggie and Becka to practice. Harry quickly learned, also, and all three learned to read music easily. Maggie and Becka loved the big old upright Beckwith piano. It was a "player" piano, and had many rolls of music for endless amusement. The pedals of the piano had to be "pumped" as the rolls turned and produced the lovely melodies. Becka thought it "magic." She and Maggie enjoyed this time together. As Maggie played, the twins and Becka would sing. Their trio of voices blended well, and they were often asked to sing for the church services.

Will had graduated from high school and after taking some classes at the local technical school, got a job at the tannery. It was very hard and smelly work, but he was proud of his job, and happy to be making his own money. He arranged for the family to visit the tannery to see what kind of job he had. Ben declined to go, but Liz, Maggie and the twins, as well as Becka were anxious to go see where Will worked…and Becka would always remember that visit.

The smell was horrendous! The large skins of the cattle would be scraped and put into vats where they were "seasoned," then pulled from the vats of chemicals to be scraped and softened again. The smell from that single visit clung to the hair and clothing of the entire family, and everyone could think of nothing but taking a shower once they reached home.

True, while eventually the hides would be made into beautiful leather garments or furniture, the tannery, in only processing the leather, did not manufacture the end products. Finally her turn in the shower, Becka stood long under the cleansing water knowing she would always have a far greater appreciation for the effort involved whenever again wearing any garment made of leather.

As the twins grew older they were more careful about their mischief, although the mischief making continued. Ben now administered the punishment. Yes, it was prudent not to get caught; the results could be very painful. Still, the temptation was there. One Sunday morning Harry called Henry aside as they were preparing for church. The twins did not like the new young preacher. He was stiff and bossy and not at all like the older minister, Brother Rayburn.

"Look here" he said quietly, "I've got a box of red fire ants in here." Henry peeked inside at the angry red ants. Harry closed the box quickly. "How would you like to see the new preacher dance?"

Henry knew immediately what Harry meant. "Uh-huh," he giggled. "Fun!"

One of the jobs assigned to the twins at church was distributing the hymnals to each seat. This little task made it quite easy for Harry to place the small box under the preacher's chair with the lid slightly open. His timing was perfect. The new young preacher barely had time to sit down as the first hymn was played before he felt a decided stinging around his ankles.

The young man jumped up and began to "dance" around the podium! The congregation stared in surprise, some of them thinking that the new preacher had "felt the Spirit" and was jumping for joy. Ben, who had accompanied the family to church that morning, glanced down at the twins. Both boys were red-faced, trying to contain their laughter. The preacher continued to jump around, slapping at his trousers and legs. He finally ran out of the church through the side door. By this time the ants had made their way to the first row of worshipers. It was not long before the whole front row bean to dance and "get religion."

"Ants!" Someone cried, "Fire ants are all over the place!"

The entire congregation exited the church as quickly as possible. Ben grabbed both boys by their collars and marched them to the back of the church.

"Wait for me," he said to Liz, "I'll be back soon. I've got a little matter to attend to first." That night the twins ate their dinner, standing up. In fact, they were unable to sit in comfort for several days.

"Well.... it was worth it," said Harry quietly, rubbing his sore bottom. "Did you see that preacher dance? He really got religion today!" They continued to laugh through their tears, but tried not to let their Pa hear them.

They had to apologize to the whole congregation, and each Saturday morning for a month, they were required to sweep out the social hall and clean the kitchen. The greatest punishment for the twins, however, was seeing the sad look on their mother's face. They both felt so bad that they resolved not to get into mischief again. For the most part they were successful. Ben had secretly smiled to himself when he thought of the incident. Oh yes, he had pulled a few stunts like that himself when he was young.

It was toward the end of August that summer of 1930 when Becka would have her frightful dream about the fire at the home of her Aunt Charlotte. Of a frantic telephone call, and the line suddenly going dead. Of thick, swirling smoke, and the chaos of shouting people, barking dogs, and screaming livestock. Of a gigantic oak exploding into flame, and the loss of a home that had seen several generations and more than 100 years. Becka's family would be occupied for the rest of that and well into fall helping Charlotte and Frank as they tried to rebuild their lives, and adjust the terrible loss.

In 1932 when Becka was nine years old, the great Depression gripped the country. Men were out of work everywhere, and many families were hungry, unable to buy food or necessities. The local grocery stores extended credit to many families, but were unable to meet all the needs. Ben and his family were some of the ““lucky” ones. Because of Ben’s skill and knowledge of machinery, he was kept on the job to help keep the machinery in good repair at the Mill.

But the Mill was “down” now, running only as necessary to keep from going completely under. And soon Will lost his job at the tannery. But while he was sad to be out of work, he began to read many technical books and to study about engineering.

During those “hard times” many small, (and large) businesses did “go under, and local businesses were no exception. One day when Ben had stopped to pick up the groceries for the week, Mr. Barder the store owner related an all too common story.

“Don’t know if I can keep letting folks run up a tab,” he began. “You know, Ben, if it weren’t for families like yours, I’d go broke.” Worry lines deepening on his face, he finished boxing up the groceries. “Now you,” he went on, “you’re always able to pay. Some of the folks just can’t. They don’t have any money. Still,” he shook his head sadly, “I can’t let ‘em starve.”

Becka and her best friend, Hilda, often took long bicycle rides through the countryside. Saturday was their special day. Because they were only nine years old, they were not allowed to ride their bicycles very far from home. But they rode to the creek near Hilda’s home and often played in the water below the small falls. Although they were young, they often discussed things that were happening around them such as the fact that so many of their friends had fathers who were out of work, and the children were often hungry without lunches at school.

Both Hilda and Becka shared their lunches with some of the other students. One of their young friends, Laverne, had lost her father. He had died unexpectedly, and left the family with little money. Her mother worked wherever she could find work, and Laverne got a job in the little restaurant next to the school. This way La Verne was able to have a nutritious lunch each day. Becka had convinced her mother to put extra apples in her lunch pail. Both little girls had tender hearts and truly wanted to help their friends.

Hilda's father had kept his job, as had Ben. The two men were good friends. Hilda had older sisters who were in college. The older sisters were struggling, as was Maggie, to keep part time jobs and help with the expenses of a college education.

The three little girls, Becka, Hilda and Laverne were "best friends" and often discussed the things that were happening around them. One of their teachers, Mrs. Rose, was Becka's favorite. She kept National Geographic magazines in the wide windowsills at school. When the girls finished their schoolwork they were allowed to take a magazine from the window to read. Becka loved it, and told her mother she was "learning so much about everything."

Becka, Hilda and Laverne would always remember their third grade class, and the time one winter day, when the large pot bellied stove overturned, setting the room on fire! The stove had fallen right in front of the door, blocking the exit, and the young teacher, Mrs. Fitch, told the children to get up on top of their desks and walk quickly from one desk to the next until they reached the back windows. Located below ground, the room's windows opened outward toward the yard. By lifting each child and put him or her through the window out on the snowy lawn, the teacher accomplished this remarkable rescue without a single child being hurt! Only after all 35 children were safe did she climb out the window herself.

While the fire trucks arrived in time to save the building, the room was in shambles! Becka remembered that she had "saved" her beautiful satin book satchel that had been made by her mother. But there was one thing she would never forget, the sight of her friend Hilda, instead of going out the window with everyone else, take a running leap and clearing the burning stove. Then, landing in the hall outside, running down the hall shouting "FIRE!!" at the top of her lungs. Her screams alerted the whole school, and everyone exited the building as quickly as possible.

During those years there were difficult times for Maggie. Having completed high school she was now in her first year of college in Kentucky. As this college allowed students to work for their tuition, Maggie managed to get a two jobs. One was working in the library at the school, and the other was a job as tutor to students who were having trouble with math. A "math whiz," Maggie sailed through all the higher mathematics classes with ease, tutoring others in algebra, trigonometry and calculus.

During the depression while Maggie was in college, Ben put his car up on jacks and walked the four miles to work. Going to work in the morning was not so bad, but the walk home was all up hill. He was doing the work of six men, and when he came home in the evening, he was dead tired. Liz worried about him, and always had a hot supper waiting for him. Before the depression he had been working the "swing" shift, but with the Mill down, he only worked days...and was glad to get the work.

With the steady work he was able to feed his family and help keep Maggie in college. Each morning Elizabeth baked a large pan of corn bread. She fried slab bacon, slicing it into thick pieces and after frying it she put the bacon and the corn bread on the back of the large old kitchen range. She kept the food warm and handed out cornbread, bacon, and hot coffee with cream and sugar to the tired and hungry men who came to her back door.

None of the men would come into the house, but sat on the back porch or out in the yard. There was an outdoor privy near the tool shed and the men used it gratefully. They washed their hands and faces with warm soapy water Liz provided them and often asked if they could do some work for her in thanks for the food. While she usually declined, feeling that they were weary enough with their travels, lack of sleep, and hunger, some of the men did rake leaves, or clean out the barn. Sometimes, older men, with gray hair and beards would ask if they could "just sleep for a little while in the warm barn." On these occasions Liz would send the twins to fetch blankets and pillows to make the old men (old before their time) feel comfortable.

One older man stayed for several weeks. He slept in the barn at night and helped with the chores around the house during the day. His name was Carl, and he was such a help to Liz that she hated to see him travel on. He had a harmonica, and at night his sweet lonely melodies could be heard floating across the farmyard. On one of those evenings Ben learned that Carl had no family, having lost his wife to cancer during the Great War, and that they had never had any children. He "had a brother somewhere" he'd told Ben, but didn't know where.

Becka helped her mother as best she could. She was curious about these men, these strangers, and asked Liz who they were and where they came from. Elizabeth smiled a tired smile and said, "These men are the 'Bonus Army' honey."

"Bonus Army?"

"Uh huh. They are veterans of the Great War. They come from all over the country and most are traveling to

Washington, D.C. to try to collect their 'bonuses' from the Government." Liz went on with what she was doing.

"But what's a bonus?" the child persisted.

"The bonus is money, sweetheart, about $900, I think."

Becka's eyes widened. A loaf of bread was only a dime, and she'd heard her father say he could buy a whole car for $200!!!

"Could daddy get in the Bonus Army," she asked hopefully, "then we could get $900, too?"

"No honey," her mother answered, "the men who are walking to Washington to get that money had to go through a whole war for it, and no amount of money is worth that. It happened way back before you were born, and I praised God during that awful time that your daddy didn't have to go.

"No," she went on, "the government owes them the money, but they're not supposed to get it until, well, let me see…not until you're 23 years old."

Becka's eyes widened further. "But that's just forever!"

Her mother smiled. "I know it must seem that way, but that money is supposed to be for their retirement."

"Retirement?"

"Uh huh. Money for when they're old and aren't working anymore. But the problem is, they're out of work now… these men and millions of others…and they're hungry now…and their families are starving now." Yes, Elizabeth thought to herself, $900 would solve a lot of problems for everyone.

"So they want it now," Becka stated with finality. She looked at her mother's worried face. "Will the government give them the bonus?" She asked.

There was a knock on the door. "I surely hope so," Liz said, turning to answer the door.

The gentle knock came from yet another bedraggled and hungry man seeking food, or simply a place of temporary rest.

History would show that the men of the Bonus Army would not receive their money from Washington. Instead, federal troops would be called out, the men would be ordered to disperse, and their "Hooverville" shantytown would be burned to the ground.

Life was indeed hard during the Great Depression, and everywhere throughout the area "kitchen gardens" were planted. These gardens supplied the families with fresh vegetables, and any excess was canned for the winter months.

Liz and the children planted a large kitchen garden. They grew beans, tomatoes, yams, potatoes, corn and peas. The apple trees furnished fresh fruit and there was a plum tree and grape vines growing on the wire fence. Livestock was destined for the table, and Liz saved all scraps for Mr. Cole's pigs. She gave strict orders to Becka and the twins that they were not to make "pets" of the chickens.

"Those chickens are for eggs and meat," she would admonish the children, "they are not pets,"

Chicken dinners were a staple for the family. Several times a year she allowed a hen to "set" so there would always be an ample supply of baby chicks coming along. Becka loved to feed the chickens, and could not help making friends with some of them.

One of her favorites was "Big Red" the rooster. When Becka brought the chicken feed to the coop he would run "talking" to her, and she would mimic his sounds and "talk" to him. Becka was seldom spanked, but when Elizabeth caught her petting the rooster, she put Becka across her knee and paddled her.

"But Mommy," Becka said through her tears, "Big

Red loves me. The chickens all love me...and I love them!" She cried. "You just can't kill 'em and eat 'em. I won't eat, I won't."

Elizabeth, despairing of ever making the child understand, knew something had to be done. "From now on, you are not to feed the chickens, do you understand?"

Becka could be a very stubborn child, and refused to eat chicken, no matter how many scoldings or even spankings came her way. And she knew that chickens came from eggs...so she refused to eat eggs! Elizabeth had to disguise the eggs and chicken meat in casseroles in order to get the needed protein into Becka's diet.

The depression years were tough times for the whole family. The twins caught nasty colds during the winter and later had to have their tonsils removed. There was no insurance and it was a big expense for Ben. Maggie worried that the family would have too hard a time keeping her in college, and wrote home that she wanted to quit and get a job. Both Ben and Liz wrote to her to stay in college. The twins would always remember the day they received a package in the mail. Maggie had sent them a little gift to cheer them up. They were delighted to find small boxes of chocolate covered cherries!

Maggie finished the first year with a provisional certificate to teach in elementary school. After that she taught during the winter and went to college during the summer until she had her full degree. That first year she was able to teach third grade at the local elementary school. She had sixty children in her class, sitting double in wide seats with broad double desks. She was paid sixty dollars a month—one dollar a month for each child! At twenty years old, Maggie was thin and frail from the strain of constant studies and the added burden of so many children in the class.

She would often have "crying jags" as the twins called them. The least little thing seemed to "set her off" into a weeping, sobbing "huddle." Finally Liz insisted on taking Maggie to see a doctor, and was told that Maggie was on the verge of a "nervous breakdown." That summer, Ben and Liz insisted that she stay home and rest to protect her health. Maggie consented, but only if she was able to take some of her college courses through correspondence studies. The college was agreeable and Maggie was able to get much needed rest.

By 1935 Ben had been given a raise and was able to drive the car again, much to Liz's relief. She did not want him walking home after putting in ten hours of hard work. That same year Will had been able to obtain a job with the shipyards in Maryland, a job that paid more than his job at the tannery. There he had met a beautiful girl, fallen in love, and eloped. Needless to say, Ben and Liz were not very happy with him for eloping, but, they liked his new young wife. They were sad to see him move to Maryland, but were happy he had a good job, and they both hoped and prayed that this move would be a happy one for Will and his wife, even tho both were very young.

The whole country was struggling to come out from under the Depression. Now, with a new President in Washington and social welfare programs established, there were "make jobs" for the thousands of men still desperately in need of work, and, ever so gradually the gloom of the depression years was finally beginning to lift.

It was 1936 and war clouds were gathering over Europe and in the Far East. By 1938 war was generally seen as inevitable. Now it would not be the welfare programs, nor the "make-do" jobs that would finally bring the country out of the depression. Rather, it would be the gearing up of factories for the production of arms and ammunition. The tanks and guns, and the many jobs in those factories, for both men and women would lift the country back to it's feet.

Although America and the world was not yet at war, it was fast becoming a wartime economy. Many thousands of men had traveled to Washington, D.C. get their World War One bonuses and had been sadly disappointed. Refused their bonuses, and literally chased out of the Nation's capital they were left penniless, returning home any way they could. There was considerable resentment...bitter resentment on the part of these men, and there was now a distrust of Government that was to last a lifetime.

Now, many of the thousands of men who had made up the so-called Bonus Army were finally able to find work in the factories. Yes, they were older, but they were experienced, and found work easily. However, this erased neither the bitter feelings nor the suffering for which they felt the government to be responsible.

Of course, at their young age, Becka and the twins were unaware for the most part, of the tremendous events taking place in their own country as well as throughout the world. Maggie, the oldest, was the most aware and spoke of these things to her parents. She read the papers and tried to keep her students informed as well as she was able. She faithfully reported the news as she understood it, and engaged in discussion about some of the world affairs with other teachers. Many of the teachers were worried.

Some of them were very afraid that the U.S. would "get into this mess" and were adamant that the country should "mind our own business" and stay out of it. "All this 'lend-lease' is just another way of getting us involved," said one of the male teachers. "But we need to lend our support to our allies," answered another teacher.

Maggie was confused and uneasy. She didn't like the way the news was going. She worried about her young brothers, Harry and Henry, as well as Will. She worried about her boy friend, Johnny. When jobs were so scarce during the depression, and before things began to pick-up economically, Johnny had joined a program called the CCC (The Civilian Conservation Corps). He had been put to work, with many other young men, doing all kinds of community projects.

Johnny enjoyed the work, the comradeship of the other young men, and had a feeling that he was "doing a good thing" for his country. Maggie received letters from him quite often. She loved getting his letters. He wrote of what he was doing and described in hilarious detail some of the things that happened in the CCC camp. He always had a last paragraph especially for her. This paragraph she kept to herself. It was full of his feelings for her and how much he missed her. Ben had long since given up on his feeling of distrust for Johnny and now voiced no objections to Maggie dating him. When Johnny came home on furlough from the CCC, he and Maggie went out to movies and other activities, without Becka as a "chaperone."

"Are you in love with Johnny?" Becka asked Maggie one evening as Maggie was preparing to go out with Johnny.

"Yes, I guess I am," said Maggie, combing her long, silky brown hair. "Don't tell Ma or Pa, but he asked me to marry him. And I said yes."

She smiled at Becka, knowing her sister could keep a secret, and had no fear about telling her anything. Becka was older now, a teenager, and the two girls had become real friends for the first time. There was no longer the big sister, "I'm the boss" attitude from Maggie. She and Becka were almost, if not quite, on an equal basis.

"I like Johnny," said Becka simply. "I think Mama and

Daddy like him fine now," she continued. "Maybe you should tell them. I really think they'll be happy for you."

"Well, I just don't know," said Maggie slowly. "Dad won't like it 'cause Johnny doesn't have a 'real' job, you know. The CCC is just a temporary thing."

However, Johnny had taken classes in high school that gave him skills for office work. He planned to get a job as a bookkeeper or accountant when he left the CCC, and had written Maggie that he wanted to get married as soon as he returned home.

"I want a church wedding," Maggie told Becka. "John and I want you to be maid of honor," she smiled, giving her a hug.

"Wow," said Becka. "I'd love to be your maid of honor. You should tell Mom soon, so she can start making our dresses!"

Becka's eyes sparkled as she contemplated a new long dress for the wedding. When Johnny arrived that evening to take Maggie out, he encountered Benjamin sitting on the front porch reading the paper. It was a beautiful summer evening, and the sun was still shining at nearly 7 P.M.

"Good evening, Mr. Young." Johnny said politely. "The news is not very good these days, is it?" Ben put the paper aside and reached out to shake the young man's offered hand.

"Hello, John" Ben said, "No, the news isn't good. I'm worried about what's going on over there in Europe."

The two men talked for a few more minutes, then Johnny cleared his throat, and said nervously, "I'll be getting out of the CCC soon. I have a job waiting for me, and uh," he stammered, "uh, well, I want to marry your daughter, Maggie," he finished in a rush.

"Oh, you do, do you?" Ben replied, suppressing a smile.

"Well, what does Maggie say about it?"

Johnny let out a sigh, "Well, Sir, she said yes…that she did!"

"I'll tell you what, young man," said Ben, "Let's wait until you have that job you're talking about. Then we can talk about this business of getting married to my daughter."

At that Ben picked up his newspaper paper and Johnny knew he'd been dismissed. By this time Maggie had already talked to her mother about the wedding plans, and after some persuasion on Liz's part, Ben had consented to the wedding as well…just soon as John's service was over in the CCC. Of course Ben hadn't let Johnny know of this. Better, he thought, to wait on that last part.

It was a lovely wedding, with Maggie in a white dress, Becka, as Maid of Honor, wore a long pearl pink gown. The twins were "best men" and Ben was proud as he walked his lovely daughter down the isle. Brother Will acted as usher. He had managed to come home for the wedding. Elizabeth and Ben hosted a reception for the young couple at their home after the wedding. It was a beautiful early afternoon affair, with ribbons decorating the branches of the old apple trees in the yard. The whole family as well as close friends were there to congratulate the happy couple. And as usual, in Ben and Elizabeth's home, any celebration was a opportunity for the family to sing. The newlyweds joined in as joyful and romantic songs were sung.

CHAPTER SIX

The Twins – 1941

ON DECEMBER 7th the Japanese bombed Pearl Harbor! These momentous events changed not only Ben and Elizabeth's lives, but also the lives of millions of people around the world. Everyone who was old enough to be aware of the significance of this act, remembered for the rest of their lives, just where they were, and what they were doing, when they first heard the dreadful news.

During the past year, many of Harry and Henry's friends had dropped out of school to join the armed services. However, the twins were planning to stay in college, with Harry wanting to become a doctor, and Henry wanting to be a reporter, or writer for a newspaper.

These plans were shattered as the news of the Pearl Harbor bombing swept the country.

Many people in the U.S. didn't know where Pearl Harbor was, and were unaware of any tension or problems between the U.S. and Japan. To many, this came as a complete shock.

Ben, however, was quite aware of the growing tension. He and Liz stayed well informed of world events, and although they did not voice their fears and concerns to the family, they were nevertheless concerned and worried.

That afternoon, December 7th, Harry and Henry had taken Becka with them to a movie in Ashland. They were enjoying bags of popcorn, laughing at the movie, when the house lights came on, the movie was stopped, and a man came running down the isle shouting, "We've been bombed by the Japs! We've been bombed by the Japs!!"

Harry grabbed the man's arm. "Where?" he asked,

"Some place in the Pacific Ocean on the Hawaiian Islands. The news said it was a naval base called Pearl Harbor," the man told Harry.

Both Harry and Henry knew where this base was located, and felt, as did most Americans, a sense of outrage and anger.

"I'm going to join the Navy!" said Harry. "With the classes I've taken in pre-med, I may be able to get in as a Medic."

"It's the Army for me!" said Henry. "I would like to be a war-correspondent, or work for a military newspaper. I really don't care, I just want to get started as soon as possible."

The three young people were driving home in Harry's car. Becka sat quietly listening to her older brothers. She loved them both very much and was proud of them, and their desire to "serve their country."

"You know," she said quietly, "Mom and Dad won't want you joining up. They want you to finish college."

"Yeah, we know, Sis," said Henry, "but we just can't wait until we're drafted. We want to pick our own service."

Becka nodded her head in agreement. There was really no argument. She thought the boys were right, and Mom and Dad would probably agree. Still she felt very uneasy and troubled. Her heart was beating fast and she felt the palms of her hands sweating. She had had a "dream" several weeks ago, a troubling dream of airplanes, ships and men, of screaming, blood and total destruction. When she had awakened she had been icy cold and trembling.

In the dream she could not see where the ships and planes were, and the misty "vision" faded in and out of her troubled mind. She had been having these troubling dreams more frequently during the past year. It had been several years since she had experienced any sort of "vision" or dream. She had hoped that she had out-grown them, and had talked to her parents about this. Long before, when she was a small child, she had learned to keep quiet about her "visions" and "dreams" and only confided in her parents or other family members, if she told anyone at all.

One recurring dream she kept strictly to herself. She did not confide in anyone; even Harry was not told of this particular dream. For a change, this dream was a pleasant one, and she might have discounted it altogether, had it not returned to her often. In the dream she was walking along a sandy beach, the warm surf lapped at her bare feet. Seagulls swooped and called above her head, and the salty air tasted good on her lips. She felt happy and full of vitality. She was looking for someone. She was meeting someone. The dream was never completed, as she awakened before she could "see" the one she was meeting. She felt happy when she woke up, keeping her dream to herself. She knew in her heart the dream would complete itself "one day."

Other dreams were violent, unhappy and frightening. They were filled with smoke and fire, with violence, men screaming, guns and blood. She saw tiny babies crying for their mothers, and mothers being taken away from their children. There were dank, dark rooms and barred doors. Hundreds of starving people, reaching, reaching through the bars. She awoke from these dreams, sweating and shivering and debated if she should tell her parents about them. She was sure they were happy that she had seemingly "outgrown" the dreams.

When she finally did tell her parents, they listened quietly. Ben took Becka's hand, and Liz sat next to her on the sofa.

"Your Mom and I have had the feeling that your dreams had returned," Ben began gently. "We were waiting for you to come to us," he continued in a soft voice. "We've been keeping up with the news as it's reported on the radio and we've heard that there's a 'mad man' in Germany. He's calling his armies to attack neighboring countries and he's slaughtering hundreds of Jewish people…and eliminating anyone who tries to protect them. The Germans look on him as a great leader…and we've even heard that some of them consider him a 'God.' He's an evil man, and vows to rid the 'whole world' of all those who are not of, what he calls, and the 'Arian' race."

"Who is he, Dad?" Becka asked in a frightened voice.

"His name is Adolph Hitler," said Liz. "He's the dictator of Germany and in control of a mighty army." Elizabeth hugged Becka, and Ben squeezed her hand.

"We feel," said Ben, "that these dreams are very real. In some way we do not understand why God is giving you these 'visions' of what is going on over there. I don't believe," he continued," that you are the only one given these 'insights.' Many men in places of high authority have 'foreseen' these events. They have spoken up and warned the government of the dangers of such a man as Hitler. Some of them have been listened to, but most are being ignored." He shook his head.

"But Dad" said Becka with an anxious voice, "I'm just a teen-aged girl. What can I do?" she asked, bursting into tears.

Elizabeth, with tears streaming down her own face, hugged Becka to her. She looked at Ben over the girl's bowed head. Ben saw the misery in his wife's face, and reflected his own concern and helplessness.

Later that evening, Beulah found Becka sitting alone in her room. She knocked softly and asked Becka if she could come in. "Sure," said Becka, and made room for Beulah on the side of her small bed.

"Chile," Beulah said, her voice dropping into the melodic dialect of the Deep South, "I 'tole you once afore, Chile, you been given a gift, a gift from God." When Becka shook her head and turned away, Beulah continued. "Don't you go shakin' yo head at the Almighty. He knows what He doing. We ain't knowing enough to question Him."

She pulled Becka to her and put the girl's head on her shoulder and cradled her, as she when she was a small child. "You come on, now" Beulah continued, "You jest listen to your old Aunt Beulah. The Lord's ways are mysterious ways. We can't always tell what they mean. We jest haf to have faith and believe in Him." She lowered her voice and whispered in Becka's ear. "Just you pray about it, little honey. He hears you. You just pray and He'll answer you in His own time."

Becka looked up at Beulah. She had great love and affection for this good woman. She hugged Beulah, and said "I will, Aunt Beulah, I promise I will."

Becka did pray. And although she was given no "answers" she somehow felt better. Her shoulders felt lighter, as though a heavy load had been lifted from them.

One evening, several days after the December 7th

event, Harry called Becka aside. "Hey, Sis, want to go for a walk after dinner?"

"Sure," said Becka.

As soon as supper was eaten and the dishes washed, Becka and Harry put on warm jackets and left the house for one of their special walks together. It was something the two had enjoyed since growing up and away from their imaginative games that had so enthralled them as children. As the two walked briskly along the snowy street, the light snow stuck to their hair and clothing. It was early evening and there was not much traffic. They came to the park and walked across the footbridge.

Becka laughed and said, "This is where that big old crawdad got hold of my toe."

"Yeah," laughed Harry, "I wish I'd seen that." He gave Becka a hug. "Well, you liked old Johnny from the first, didn't you? Becka nodded, smiling.

She had liked Johnny. She felt, even as a child, those many years ago, that Johnny really loved Maggie, and would be O.K. for her.

"I'm glad they got married. I'm gonna miss them when they move to the Army base where they're sending John."

The two walked on in silence for a few more minutes. They felt a closeness when together, a closeness that didn't need conversation. They were comfortable in each other's company, and shared a rare brother-sister friendship that was a loving bond between them.

"I did it, Sis," Harry said simply. "I joined the Navy and have to report for duty in three weeks."

Becka took Harry's gloved hand. "Have you told Mom and Dad? And does Henry know?" she asked.

"Not yet," answered Harry, squeezing Becka's hand. "I plan to tell Henry first, then announce it at dinner tomorrow."

"I'll bet Henry has already been looking into joining the Army," said Becka. "Oh, Henry, things will never be the same around here. But I guess that's just the way things turn out. So much is happening, everywhere!"

Becka shook her head and looked around at the lovely trees, the gently falling snow, and the swiftly flowing creek beneath the bridge. She looked up into her brother's face, and her eyes filled with tears. Harry brushed her cheek with his gloved hand. His own eyes were misting.

He cleared his throat. "Life never stands still, you know. And boy, for us it's on a fast track!" He pulled Becka into a hug and continued. "Things will be changing for you, too, Becka. You already have thought about it, I know. What are your plans?"

Becka wiped her eyes on her scarf and managed a smile. "Yes," she said "I've been thinking of taking a Civil Service exam and going to Washington D.C. to work, if I can get a job up there."

"That sounds exciting," Harry said. "I hope you can." "I've finished my business classes and I think I can pass the Civil Service exam," Becka continued. "A man came into the classroom the other day and handed out the exams."

She turned to look out across the footbridge at the bubbling creek and the wooded area beyond. It is so beautiful here, she thought. I love this place in the winter.

"I know, Harry, that I'll pass." Becka continued. "I also know that things will never be the same. We, you and Henry, and I, we will all leave this beautiful town. We will leave our parents, and that's the way it should be, I guess."

"Hey," said Harry, "Don't be sad, Sis. Frankly, I'm very excited. You know me. I'm always up for something new!

And believe me, what's coming up for us will be new, and different, and I guess, dangerous."

He pulled off his wool cap and shook his blond curly head. The snow was falling more steadily and the flakes were clinging to their clothes and hair.

"I guess we'd better get back before we turn into snow people," laughed Becka.

They were young, and in love with life. Their eyes sparkled at the thought of these new and exciting times anticipated in the future. Although Becka foresaw dark shadows she pushed them to the back of her consciousness. Harry was feeling only exhilaration. He had been accepted into the Navy as an Ensign, with the promise of working as a medic, perhaps on a battleship. He just couldn't believe his good luck! The two walked home through the falling snow, comfortable in their companionship, each wrapped in their own thoughts.

It was dark by the time they reached home, although it was only 6 p.m. The winter days were dark and short. Elizabeth watched as the two removed their heavy winter jackets, boots, gloves and caps. Her heart swelled with love for her children. They are so young, and yes, beautiful. Harry with his excited young face, full of anticipation; Becka, thoughtful, yet anticipating new things.

"Oh God," she prayed silently, "Take care of them, wrap your protecting arms about them, and keep them safe. Bring them home. And oh God, help me to let them go gracefully."

Her tears were close to the surface, and she swallowed a lump in her throat. Elizabeth swallowed again and said "How would you two like some hot cocoa and a piece of apple pie?"

"Would we!" Harry answered for them both. "Just lead

us to the table!

"Did I hear someone say apple pie?" Ben asked as he walked into the kitchen. Elizabeth laughed and cut another generous piece of pie for Ben and a piece for herself.

They all sat together at the old round table in the kitchen. Although the talk was light and did not touch on the things that were in each of their minds, the knowledge of the impending separations hung above them like a floating somber cloud. The twins were so excited that they could hardly contain themselves. It was going to be the greatest "adventure" of their lives, and they were looking forward to it. The grinding work, lack of sleep, the hardships, the danger, death and miseries that are all a part of war, were far from their minds.

Ben and Elizabeth knew, and Becka knew, also, because of her dreams but they kept their thoughts to themselves. Nothing they could say or do would change the minds of the twins. They were determined, as were thousands of other young men in their community to "get in there and serve their country." They were, as Tom Brokaw would write many years later, part of the Greatest Generation.*

Both Harry and Henry, due of their educational background and keen intelligence, were accepted as officers in the military. Harry enlisted as an Ensign in the Navy, to serve, after training "somewhere in the Pacific sector." Henry enlisted in the Army. He would serve, after initial training, as a war correspondent.

To the twins, it seemed almost too good to be true. It was exactly what they wanted. Both young men were to report for duty in three weeks. The impending separation from their parents and family did not seem to bother them as much as it did their parents and Becka. If the twins were sad about leaving, they kept their feelings to themselves.

Elizabeth and Ben, as well as Becka, "put on happy faces" and Liz planned a going-away party for the boys. The party was a big success. Many of the friends of the twins, as well as family members came to help celebrate. Aunt Charlotte and Uncle Frank and their boys Charles and Frank, Jr. came, laden with baked goodies and a beautiful sugar cured ham. Aunt Cora and Uncle Henry came with knitted scarves for the twins, and homemade butter cookies. Ben's older brother and his wife drove all the way from Virginia, their own sons having already joined the Army and now serving in the Philippines. Harry and Henry had invited special girl friends who came, teary-eyed and clinging, eliciting promises from the twins that they would "write every day" and "stay true-blue."

The small frame house on the hill would not see a party like this one for many years.

Outside it was bitter cold. Wind howled around the eves and snow covered the ground. Inside, the fire blazed happily on the hearth and smiles wreathed the faces of the young people.

Still, tears shimmered in back of the eyes of the older members of the family. Ben's brother Tom had served during World War One and had been wounded in France. His spine crooked, he would walk with a limp for the rest of his life.

Holding no youthful expectations of "glamour" or grand "adventures," neither Tom nor his wife were strangers to the miseries of war. Both of their sons, aged 20 and 22, had been sent to the Philippines and were now serving under Gen. Wainwright's command. The Philippines had also been bombed shortly after Pearl Harbor was hit, but their sons had managed to get word to their parents that they were safe "for now."

Regardless, Tom and his wife were very worried. How could they not? According to the meager news coming from that area, it was a volatile and dangerous place to be. Ben and Tom managed to find a quiet place to talk during the party, but did not discuss or voice their fears to the young people present.

The young people had gathered in the living room around the old upright piano. Harry had his guitar and Henry the violin. Becka played the piano, and the young voices rose in happy unison. They sang songs that were popular at the time, and enjoyed popcorn, candy, cookies, and Ben's special apple cider (slightly fermented). It was a boisterous, happy crowd that did not break up until after midnight.

Several of the young men who had consumed slightly more than their share of the cider, bunked out on the floor to spend the night. Ben and Liz made sure there were pillows and blankets available, as the night was extremely cold. Most of the older couples had left earlier, and the out-of-town relatives were spending the night in the extra rooms available. Becka took a cot in her parents' room, and the twins were bunking together on the sofas in the living room.

The little frame house was full to over-flowing that cold winter night in January, 1942. Liz had taken down all the Christmas decorations in preparation for this party. She and Becka had stored the things away, both wondering, although not aloud, what the next Christmas would be like, with the boys off in the Service. Everything would be so different.

Liz had had tears in her eyes as she wrapped the special ornaments that had been hand-made by the twins. There were small hand carved camels, sheep and cows, with a tiny manger holding the Christ child, and Mary and Joseph standing close by. Harry had carved a beautiful angel to preside over the entire manger scene. Liz wrapped these precious figures and gently laid them in a special box that would protect them until next year.

While mother and daughter were working together, they had discussed Becka's plans. Becka told her mother about the civil service exam, and her plans to go to Washington, D.C. to work, if she passed the exam. She did not tell her mother that somehow she "knew" that she would pass and would leave, soon, to work in the Nation's capital. Becka also knew that her parents wanted her to stay near home, perhaps get married and settle down.

While one of the young men asleep on the floor in the living room had been Becka's special "date" the evening of the party, Becka was not interested in getting married, not yet, and not to George. He was a "nice guy" she thought, but he was not for her. Besides, she had other things to do first, and was almost as excited as the twins about leaving home. After all, she was going to an exciting job in Washington.

The next morning after the going-away party for the twins, Liz slipped out of bed before the sun managed to peek through the high thin clouds. The earth was covered with a beautiful blanket of snow. It clung to the trees and covered all unsightly garden barrels, hay mounds and hedgerows with a silvery blanket of white. Liz put on her heavy winter coat, gloves and boots and ventured out into the unmarked snow to feed the chickens. The great chow dog, Brutus, raised his head from his warm bed beneath the shed and came to accompany Liz as she made her "rounds."

Liz patted his warm shaggy head and the dog looked up at her and wagged his tail in appreciation. "Come on, old fellow," Liz said to the dog, "let's get back inside and get breakfast started. We have a whole house full of hungry folks."

She removed her heavy winter things and as the dog shook himself, she laughed and wiped his wet feet. Brutus was part of the family and always stayed close to Liz when it was possible for him to do so. The two entered the kitchen to find Becka and Ben already there. They had made the coffee, and Ben was putting out the bacon and eggs and preparing to make toast.

One by one, the houseguests found their way to the kitchen. The aroma of coffee, bacon and eggs was irresistible. Each was served hot rolls with apple butter, bacon and scrambled eggs, apple juice and hot coffee. There was also hot cereal – cream of wheat, grits, or oatmeal if anyone wanted it. Liz prided herself on the fact that no one should leave her house hungry!

When George, Becka's "date" came into the kitchen, he quietly asked Becka if she would take a walk with him after breakfast.

"Sure," said Becka, "but I need to help Mom clean up the kitchen first."

"That's fine," said George, "I'll help too."

The two young people scooted Liz and Ben out of the kitchen after everyone was finished, cleared the dishes and cleaned up. Soon they were finished and the kitchen was spotless.

"Come on, George," Becka said, "let's go for our walk before it starts to snow again."

They walked through the park and over the footbridge, following the winding road to the top of the hill. The view of the Ohio River, and the wooded valley spread out below them. It was beautiful, covered with snow, the crystals sparkling in the early morning sunlight. A cold north wind teased their faces, turning their noses and cheeks a bright pink. As they looked out over the broad Ohio River they saw a slow-moving barge as it made its way west down the Ohio toward the Mississippi River. Becka began to hum an old campfire song she had learned as a child.

As she hummed, George reached into his pocket and got his harmonica. "Sing the words," he urged Becka.

"O.K." she said, and began to sing the old song as George played the melody on the harmonica.

George had removed his right mitten and pulled Becka's left glove off in order to hold her hand. His hand was warm and he massaged Becka's cold fingers.

"I wanted to talk to you," he said in a serious voice. "I've joined the Marines, and will be leaving in a few weeks. Will you write to me? I know it's too early for us to talk about getting serious about each other. But, you see," he continued, "I uh, I think I'm in love with you."

Becka took a long time to answer him. "George" she said, "I'll write to you, and if, after the war, we still feel we want to continue seeing each other, well, I guess so."

She smiled up at him and squeezed his hand. George pulled her close and kissed her. She didn't pull away, but her kiss was more like a brother and sister kiss, and he did not try to deepen the embrace.

"O.K." he said. "That's fair enough, I guess. I just want to know I have 'a girl back home." He laughed and hugged her again, without the kiss.

As it turned out, all three young men, Harry, Henry and George left for their respective branches of the military within two weeks of the party. Harry went to O.C.S. in the Navy, Henry to O.C.S in the Army, and George to M.C.R.D. in San Diego, Calif.

After initial training, Henry was shipped to join Eisenhower's command in the European sector. He was very pleased to be realizing his dream to become a war correspondent. He joined a team of newsmen who were as close to the front lines as possible. This team reported the war as they saw it, but they had no words to describe some of the horror they witnessed, and in which they were sometimes involved.

This green young boy, having only recently left Kentucky, quickly became a tough, steel nerved man with a hardened shell covering his sensitive soul. His eyes lost their innocence, and lines appeared around his mouth and on his brow. Yet, Henry liked what he was doing. He was glad he was one of the men who were reporting to the world the progress of the war.

The reports were not good during the first months of his duties. However, his reporting was true to facts, and sometimes censored by his superiors, as they did not wish to make it sound as though the Allies were losing battles.

Henry received a Silver Star for bravery. Running, under fire, he dragged a wounded soldier to safety. For wounds received during the same action, Henry was also awarded the Purple Heart.

He was sent to a field hospital to have the bullet removed from his left shoulder and was out of service for over a month. During this time he would write several thought-provoking and insightful articles of correspondence to the New York Times and other leading newspapers. His reports were always welcome, and he was becoming well known throughout the Western news circuit.

The wounded soldier whom he had saved was recovering in the same field hospital and Henry went to see him often. He learned the man's name was Oscar Durrah, Jr., and that he was fram small town in California called Montalvo. Having written to his mother about the young man, Liz wrote back that she believed Oscar to be the son of a young student she had taught long ago. Still living in the small California community, Liz was able to contact Oscar Sr. and they had a wonderful long conversation on the telephone, catching up on old times, and discussing their sons' experiences in the war.

"You know, Ben," Liz said after turning to her husband at the end of the telephone conversation. "It really is a small world!"

Both parents had thanked God many times that their son had been there to save Oscar's son, and that both young men were recovering from their wounds. Oscar, Jr. had been more seriously hurt, and would not be returning to active duty. As soon as it was practical to move him, he would be shipped back home, and given a medical discharge. Henry on the other hand, was not seriously wounded and would find himself back on the front lines within a few weeks.

The twins had kept up their correspondence with each other as well as possible. Harry was serving on a battleship in the South Pacific. He had been in combat and had been able to use his medical skills to great advantage. He had not been wounded, but had been in enemy fire and treated other young men who were badly hurt. Some of the sea battles had been a "living hell" he had written Henry. He did not, however, write of this to his parents or his sisters. The twins often wrote to their older brother Will, who was serving in a civilian capacity in the shipyards. He was one of the civilian shipbuilders, and very essential to the war effort.

Com. Reynolds

Becka, Gwen, Edna
Roomates

Dressed for Work

Winter 1944

CHAPTER SEVEN

Washington D.C. 1942 – 1944

THE CIVIL service exam for secretarial positions in the Nation's capital proved to be easy for Becka, and two weeks after taking the exam she received a telegram from the Navy Department in Washington D.C. She had been offered a job opportunity! It was in the Plans Coordination Department on Constitution Ave in Washington, and, the notice instructed her to report for work by the first week of February!

She was very excited and happy. Although she was sad to leave her parents, she wanted this new experience. Liz and Ben helped Becka to get ready for the move. It was a cold winter, with snowy and unsettled weather. Maggie had friends living in Washington in a boarding house in the northeastern part of the city. She had written them about a room for Becka, and it was arranged. Housing, of any kind, was extremely scarce. Becka, as well as Liz and Ben felt happy that she could find this place.

She took the train to Washington from Ashland. It was snowing and very cold the evening she arrived at the station but she managed to get her bags into a waiting cab and gave the cabby the address of the boarding house. It seemed to Becka, on that first night in Washington, and on that first cab ride, that everything in Washington was built "in circles," and by the time she arrived at the boarding house she was thoroughly disoriented.

As she paid the cabby she asked him, "Can you please tell me if this is east or west of the Capital?"

The cabby laughed, saying simply, "it's north!"

Becka met the other boarders and quickly became friends with the girls who shared her room. There were four girls to a room and although the room was large, it was very crowded. One of the young women she shared the room with was the sister of Will's wife. Her name was Gwinnie and she and Becka felt that they had much in common. Mrs. Johnson, the landlady, cooked all their meals, cleaned their bathrooms, the halls, and the kitchen. The boarders were expected to care for their own "space."

Becka, who was accustomed to her mother's delicious cooking, had a hard time adjusting to Mrs. Johnson's bland meals. She had never tasted lamb, and curried lamb did not appeal to her southern taste buds.

Her new job at the Navy Dept. was to be the "evening shift." That meant she had to be at work at 4 p.m. and work until eleven thirty each evening. When she boarded the streetcar on Constitution Ave. each night there were plenty of other people around. However, when she got off at the corner, nearest her house, it was pitch dark and she had to walk a full block to the boarding house. The streetlights were dim and the street filled with shadows.

On the second week of Becka's work she got off the

streetcar and started down the dark and shadowy street. She felt very small and also very alone. Her senses were alert; she felt an unease that warned of danger. Looking around she saw that large hedges grew near the sidewalk, so she walked to the center of the street. There was no traffic and the street was quiet. Few lights burned from windows and shades were drawn and windows closed because of the cold.

Becka took the house key out of her purse and held it in her hand. When she reached the boarding house she ran as fast as she could toward the front steps. But she was not fast enough. As she reached the front walk a hand reached out and grabbed her arm, twisting her around. She tried to scream, but another hand covered her mouth. She twisted as fast as she could and brought her knee up between the man's legs. He grunted and released his hold on her arm. As he did so, she used her key to punch him in the eye! All the while she was screaming at the top of her voice. As the lights began to come on in the houses around them, the man cursed, gave Becka a hard shove, and ran down the street as fast as his legs could carry him.

Shaken but unhurt, Becka called the police as soon as she was safely inside. They asked her a few questions over the phone, and told her to "file a report" the next day. As Becka lay in bed that night and early morning, unable to sleep, she felt a sense of betrayal and lack of trust for the police. She realized that the police would have had only a small chance of "catching the varmint," but she thought they could have at least made an effort!

Later that day as she left for work, she stopped at the police station to make the report. She received no further communication from the police. When she arrived at the office that afternoon she related her experience to Ensign

Haulk, her boss.

"Hey," he said, "you need someone to be with you on that walk home. I know a girl, about your age who is looking for a place to live." Ensign Haulk looked around the room and continued, "There she is. Oh Miss Spencer, will you come over here, please?" And he motioned for a young woman at a desk nearby to join them.

Becka was introduced to Miss Edna Spencer. She was a pretty girl with dark brown hair and brown eyes. She had a nice smile and a twinkle in her eyes.

"I'll let the two of you get acquainted. Miss Spencer, I think you'll like what Miss Young has to tell you." He smiled and walked away.

The two young women talked for a few minutes, and Edna said she would be delighted to move to the boarding house. Becka told her there was an opening where the two girls could share a room together. The girls became "best friends" and would cherish that friendship for the years to come. They felt safer walking home from the streetcar together. They continued to walk down the center of the street, and to carry their keys, as "weapons" each night.

Working the "night shift" gave Becka and Edna time to explore their wonderful city of Washington during the hours before they had to report for work. The City was enchanting to the girls. So much to see and do. And the men! All those gorgeous men in uniform – and most of them looking for girlfriends!

Becka and Edna had dates every Saturday and Sunday. They double-dated for movies, concerts, picnics in the beautiful Rock Creek Park, and formal dances at the Officer's Clubs. Becka and Edna shopped for formal gowns spending hours trying to find shops that were in their income bracket.

The girls also attended church together. One Sunday morning when they were all dressed up, they walked outside the boarding house to the long walk to the street. Edna had a habit of swinging her arms. As she swung her right arm she felt something wet hit her sleeve, and immediately something wet hit her left arm as well. "Oh, darn!" she said disgustedly, as she surveyed her pretty jacket. A couple of seagulls had "bombed" her, and bombed her good! Her jacket had to be removed and replaced with a clean one.

Becka laughed and said, "Those seagulls are probably on the payroll of the Japanese!"

Although Becka and Edna dated a lot of young men, they were never promiscuous. The girls soon found out that there were two kinds of dates, those who "wanted one thing only" and those who respected them for their values. The girls were not prudish, and enjoyed hugs and kisses, as long as they didn't "go too far."

One evening Becka was invited to a formal dinner-dance at the beautiful Shoreham Hotel ballroom. Her date, a Naval officer, picked her up at her house. He was wearing his dress whites and looked very handsome. Becka had a new evening gown on that fitted her small figure perfectly. Rich, her date brought her a white orchid to wear on her wrist. At dinner, he ordered "pink ladies" for Becka, and a scotch and soda for himself.

"You'll like this drink," he told Becka, "It's sweet and smooth."

She did like the taste of the drink, and did not realize how much alcohol it contained. In a very few minutes she began to feel quite ill. She excused herself and fairly ran to the ladies' room. The restroom was lovely. It had marble floors, stately washstands and pink and white walls. Becka saw none of this however as she frantically looked for an open stall.

None.

She couldn't wait, and the room was full of lovely young women, dressed in their most beautiful gowns, waiting for an empty stall. Becka saw a free washstand and dashed to it just in time to lose her dinner, as well as all the "pink ladies." When she finally had emptied her stomach in the sink, she raised her head to a completely empty room. Every single young woman had dashed out of the restroom as soon as Becka became "sick!"

As sick as she felt, though, she couldn't help smiling at the way she must have looked, and how fast the room had emptied of all the fancily dressed young women. When she finally composed herself and left the restroom, she found her date, Rich, waiting for her with a concerned look on his face. He suggested that they visit the bar in the hotel. Becka at first declined, but Rich assured her that he knew the bartender and that the bartender would give her something that would settle her stomach. He gave her a concoction he called "bitters" and Becka soon felt better. She hoped she would never see any of those young women again, and she was sure she never wanted to see another "pink lady!"

Both Edna and Becka had found "special" young men that they preferred to date. Edna started seeing an officer attached to the Navy Department supply stores and she began dating Ensign Jack Adams almost exclusively. Becka also, had "someone special" but she was not supposed to date him because he was her boss. She had written to Harry that there was "some sort of silly rule" about inter-office dating. This rule didn't stop them from seeing each other; they just kept quiet about it.

Becka found that Bill Haulk, her boss, had a great sense of humor, and often played harmless tricks on those he liked. Bill smoked a pipe, and had a large collection of pipes he kept on his desk in a beautiful, round humidor. The tobacco was stored inside the canister, and the pipes were secured in brackets around the outside. One afternoon, before Bill arrived at his desk, Becka hid the humidor and pipes. When Bill came in and sat at his desk, he reached for one of his favorite pipes.

"Hey," he said, concerned. "Has someone been cleaning my desk?"

No one said a word.

He asked again, looking under his desk and in the drawers. Everyone was watching, as they knew what Becka had done. He turned to Becka whose desk was closest to his own.

"Have you seen my pipes?" he asked her.

"Why, yes, I have," she answered, deadpan. "They were so smelly that I took them home and washed them with soap and water." And she smiled sweetly at him.

"Oh no, you didn't!" and he jumped up from his desk.

"Well, yes" said Becka amiably, "I thought you'd be happy. They smell and look much better now."

She couldn't keep from grinning, and soon everyone in the office began to laugh. Bill, still not quite sure, looked around, suspecting he had been the butt of a very good prank. He had an infectious laugh, and laughed heartily at the joke. But he was also very happy to see his pipes again in their old smelly condition.

After six months of working the night shift, Becka and the other ten girls in that particular office were told that they were being reassigned to day work. Becka was assigned as a secretary to a Commander Reynolds in an office down the hall. It was then possible for Becka and Ensign William Haulk to see each other anytime, and to attend the office parties together.

Her dates with Bill were "magical." He was the first "older man" she had ever dated. She was fascinated by him, and thought Bill very handsome. He was muscular, about medium height, with dark hair, dark mustache, and soft brown eyes. He had a laugh that was hard to resist. When they were together they laughed a lot but neither Becka nor Bill wanted a serious relationship.

Bill's greatest wish was to be sent to the Pacific theatre. He felt strongly that what he was doing in Washington was "make-do" work and did not help the war effort. During the time that Becka worked for him in that particular office, he often confided in her that what she and the other office girls were doing was a useless waste of time and money.

Becka had to agree with him, as she often questioned in her own mind just what use all that paper work was doing to help "win the war." She, and the other girls were given lists of airplane parts that were being sent to airbases in the U.S. and abroad. Their job was to make an original and three copies of each part list, separate the pages, and file the original in one book file, and each of the copies in separate book files. After a month of this the "books" began to mount up and a carpenter came into the room and made a bookcase to hold the many book files.

During the six months that Becka and the other girls did this monotonous work, no one, to their knowledge, ever came into the room to check the files, or to take them anywhere. When the girls were told after six months, that they would be reassigned to day work and to other offices, Becka asked Bill if he knew "what the heck happened to all those book files?"

"They were used for the scrap paper drive!" Bill laughed.

Becka simply looked at him, shaking her head. "In my opinion," she laughed, "that's a much better use for them!"

Her new job with the Commander was much more interesting. She was allowed to take notes at special meetings and would type up these notes as reports to her boss. As a result, her accuracy and writing ability soon had her in demand at many important meetings of high-ranking staff and military personnel. She received a "security check" that, incidentally, concerned her parents, and she was cleared to handle sensitive materials.

The wartime years in Washington were exciting and full of unexpected adventures for Becka and her friends. Donna, one of her special friends was an officer in the Navy and attached to the same office where Becka was a civil employee. The two young women became good friends and often had lunch together. That spring when the cherry trees were in full bloom, the two girls were walking along the road by the reflection pool. The trees were beautiful, and it seemed so lovely and peaceful there that Becka could hardly believe that the country was at war.

The girls were laughing and talking when all of a sudden Donna came to full military "attention." Becka, surprised, looked to see whom she was saluting. Traveling on the road beside their sidewalk, a very slow moving "cavalcade" of important looking cars was passing by. Four motorcycle policemen preceded a large, black limousine, and four motorcycle police followed in its wake. As the long black sedan passed the girls, the window in the back seat slid soundlessly down and President Franklin Roosevelt, calling a temporary halt to the procession, leaned out of the window, and with his famous smile lighting his face, nodded his head at the girls and returned Donna's salute!

Becka and Friends
Washington D.C. 1943

"Good afternoon, ladies," he said in his clear distinctive voice, "the trees are beautiful, aren't they?"

"Yes, uh, Yes sir!" Donna and Becka both mumbled together.

The President smiled again and the window of the long black sedan closed as the motorcade moved on slowly and almost silently around the corridor that flanked the lovely blooming cherry trees.

"Wow," said Becka, "What do you think of that! My Mom and Dad will never believe it."

Donna, still a little awestruck, turned to Becka and said, "I've seen him before, you know. I accompanied my boss Captain Howard to the White House once. We met the President in the Oval Office. I took notes of the meeting. He can't walk, you know." She continued, "He has help standing, and is carried into the Oval Office to be seated at his desk. He doesn't allow pictures of any of this."

"Hmm," mused Becka, "I can understand why. God, I do admire that man. You know, Donna, I pray for him every day."

Donna nodded "So do I, and there are millions of other people who are praying for him, also."

The President was not the only V. I. P. the two girls were to meet accidentally. About a week later they met for lunch at the famous "tent on the green" restaurant. It was a favorite of the office workers and military stationed on Constitution Ave. The large tent restaurant was set up on the green near the Reflection Pool. The restaurant featured baked clams on the half-shell. They were delicious, always cooked to perfection and served piping hot with a delectable sauce.

Donna and Becka loved to go there for lunch. They had just picked up their orders and seated themselves, when they heard an unusual amount of murmuring and talking around them. They looked up and standing by their picnic table was General Dwight D. Eisenhower, and four of his officers. Donna quickly got to her feet, but the General motioned for her to be seated.

"May we join you ladies?" he asked, bowing politely. "You seem to have room at this table."

"Of course, Sir," Becka said quickly. She smiled at him and at the other officers, who, of course, were all smiling back at the girls.

The large tent area was equipped with long picnic tables. Every customer picked up a tray and utensils and gave their order. When the order was called, the customer went to the serving area and picked up his or her food. The General and his men followed the same routine, as did all the customers. He and his men loved those "baked clams on the half-shell" as much as most of the others in the restaurant.

The conversation at the table was lively and full of laughter. Donna was shy and did not say much, but Becka was animated and full of fun, and kept the whole group laughing.

When the men excused themselves and got up to leave, General Eisenhower turned to Becka and extended his hand. "Thank you for a most delightful lunch," he said, and squeezed her hand. Donna had risen and was saluting him. He glanced at her and smiled and gave a brief salute.

"Oh craps," moaned Donna when the men had left. "Why can't I be like you, Becka? Sometimes I just can't get my words to come out!"

But not all of Becka's experiences were so much fun. Commander Reynolds, her boss, often asked her to get the morning coffee for the weekly officers' meetings. This meant getting the orders from the men present, cream or black, sugar, and so on. She also collected the money from the men to pay for the coffee. The coffee room was down the hall and around the corner from her office.

One morning with a full tray of hot coffee, she rounded the corner and ran "smack-dab" into Admiral Nimitz! The coffee tray went skyward, the hot coffee spread itself over his beautiful uniform and Becka's pretty suit! Both girl and Admiral landed on the floor with cups and coffee, sugar and cream scattered evenly over them! They looked at each other for the space of a few seconds, and then they both began to laugh. Others in the hall ran to help them up and Becka started to apologize but the Admiral held up his hand.

"No need, young lady, he laughed. "It was entirely my fault. I should know by now to give certain areas a wide birth!"

The whole crowd that had gathered began to laugh, and Becka, with help, retrieved the cups and tray, and, although soaked in coffee, went back to the coffee room and refilled the orders. When she reappeared in the conference room, tray and coffee in hand, a loud cheer went up and a round of applause. Becka blushed bright red, for the Admiral was seated at the conference table, coffee stains and all!

About a week later, Commander Reynolds called Becka into his office and handed her an envelope. She opened it and found a lovely apology note from Admiral Nimitz, and a check to cover the cost of dry-cleaning her suit. "I had my uniform cleaned," he wrote "and everything cleaned up ship-shape, except my "battle ribbons." I do hope you have no 'battle scars' from your encounter with the Navy." Becka, who kept a journal, filed the note and the experiences of her Washington "adventures" away for safekeeping.

Becka wrote often to her parents, and to Harry and Henry as well as Maggie about the things that happened to her and around her as she lived and worked in the Capital during those momentous days of World War Two. Her older brother Will now lived in Baltimore where he was still in civilian service in the shipyards. He was a skilled worker and, for that reason did not join the military. He was married and Becka was able to visit Will and his small family several times while she lived in Washington. She enjoyed playing and reading with her two little nieces.

Lt. J.G Haulk, who had received a promotion, called Becka that summer to tell her he was being reassigned to Hawaii. They met for dinner, walked through a nearby park and as they sat down on a park bench Bill turned to Becka.

"I love you, Becka," He said looking into her eyes. "You are so special to me. I love everything about you, your eyes, your hair, your wonderful smile and sense of humor." He reached over and picked up her hand. "I wish I could put an engagement ring on your finger. But I don't think I should." He looked at her with troubled eyes. Becka sat very still. She kept her hand in his, and looked at him. There was a definite "current" flowing through their hands. Both could feel it.

"Hawaii is a long way from here," Becka said softly. "We both have some growing up to do, I think." She was not smiling and a tear trickled down her cheek. "I'm only twenty, and you are almost thirty," she continued in her soft voice. "We'll write, of course, and maybe we'll see each other after the war."

"Becka," Bill interrupted. "Don't! "I mean it, I do love you, but I can't get married, and I can't ask you to wait for me. It just wouldn't be fair to you, sweetheart. But please, don't cut your hair (she laughed at that), and please don't meet someone else and get married, please."

He pulled her to him and kissed her. His kiss was passionate and urgent. Becka's tears were streaming down her face, and Bill's eyes were moist. He took off his Navy ring and handed it to her. She held it for a few minutes, and then slowly gave it back to him.

"Thank you," she said, wiping her tears away with his large white handkerchief, "No, I can't keep it."

"Please, Becka, take it."

He held her to him, her beautiful long hair touching his face. She smelled of roses, and the soft fragrance filled him. He loved her so much, but he was not ready to get married, not yet. He wanted to wait until after the war. Things were too unsettled now, too fluid, too unsure. How could he make her understand? She was so young and had a lot of growing up to do.

"Please" he said again, urgently, "Please keep the ring. Wear it around your neck; it's too big for your little fingers, anyway." He pressed the ring into her hand, then lifted her hands and kissed her fingers, one at a time. His own eyes were moist with tears. Becka did keep the ring, but she put it away in her small chest, along with her journal and other keepsakes.

She wrote to Harry:

"I suppose it's for the best. If he had stayed here, we probably would have been engaged, maybe even married. After he left, I didn't want to date anyone else for a long time. Then I met this guy, an officer in the Navy, who is taking flying lessons at a nearby airfield. No romance here, but I've always wanted to learn to fly a plane. He tells me that there are a lot of women in the Civil Air Patrol, and if I learn to fly I could join. Wouldn't that be a blast? I'm going to do it if I can afford it. It costs fifty bucks a shot. I think I'll go for it. This Navy officer, Mark, will take me along and arrange for my lessons. Wish me luck, big brother, I just may get into the Air Force yet!

Becka signed her letters, "Your little Sis."

She did not tell her parents that she was taking flying lessons, knowing knew her Mom would worry and probably discourage her from doing this. The Galveston Airfield was about an hour's drive out in the country. Each Saturday morning Becka would pack a lunch, and the two would drive out to the field. It's "headquarters" an old farmhouse, sat apart about one-half mile distant.

The lady who owned the farm and welcomed the flyers and would-be flyers was quite a character. She had bleached-blond hair, bright blue eyes, an angular figure, and a wit as sharp as a bayonet, and could "cuss" with the best of them. She would often tease Becka for her "refined" southern accent and manners. Becka liked her, and enjoyed talking with her. She told jokes that made Becka blush, but that didn't stop her from telling them.

The men got a charge out of her, and seemed to enjoy her wit and raw humor. Becka and Mark and two other officers decided to buy their own plane. There was a small Aronca plane for sale for eight hundred dollars. If each put in two hundred dollars they could purchase the plane. Becka had managed to save some money and within two months, had the necessary amount to pay her share.

But the weekend the four were to buy the plane, a fierce storm hit the area with reported winds of over 60 miles an hour. Becka, who had had few of her "dreams" since coming to Washington, had experienced a "doozie" of a dream the night before the storm. In the dream she saw the farmhouse, battered by the wind and rain. There were portions of the roof blown away, and the trees were battered and broken. The little airplanes that were tied down on the airfield were lifted off the ground, the ropes broken and the planes smashed against each other. It was a scene of total destruction!

Becka had awakened with a chill and called Mark. Although she didn't tell him about her dream, Mark, who had been listening to the news on his radio quickly confirmed her worst fears. The airfield and the airplanes had been completely destroyed!

"My God, Becka," he said. "We just missed buying that plane. We would have been out all that money! That poor bastard who owns the plane...I hope he's got insurance!"

"I guess this means we won't be going out for any more lessons," she said, in sad agreement.

Becka loved flying. She was ready for her "solo flight" and was getting pretty good at landing without "bouncing." She knew if she could have a few more lessons she would be able to take the exam for the Civil Air Patrol. Becka thought about her dream, but the more she thought about it, the more she felt that maybe, just maybe, she should not continue on this course. She knew her parents did not want her to leave her job to join the C.A.P, and perhaps they were right.

During the war years, Washington put on a different "dress." Instead of a party frock, the city now wore a business suit. And the city was busy, very busy. Washington was full to overflowing with men and women, military as well as civilian filling the new positions needed to operate the giant war machine that was now keeping the country "free of tyranny."

Becka had a patriotic heart and truly wanted to do her part for the war effort. But war creates uncertainty. She worried constantly about her brothers, now overseas and in "harms way." And, while she enjoyed receiving letters from home and elsewhere, the underlying tone was always a re-emphasis of the horror taking place around the world.

Harry had written that he was assigned to the U.S.S.

Nicholas, a Flagship, operating in the Kula Gulf in the Pacific theatre. And Henry, as last she heard, had recovered from his wounds and was back on the front lines in France. A letter from Elizabeth informed Becka that "…so many of the young men from the Ashland area have been killed or wounded," concluding with sad news that two of her first cousins had been confirmed killed at Pearl Harbor. And George, the boy from her hometown, had written that he had survived the Battle of Midway uninjurred. "…the fight for the island was "horrendous," the letter went on, "…. but many of my buddies were killed or wounded."

In Washington the ebb and flow of the war news permeated the atmosphere. In early 1943, the news was not all good. Even though the newsreels showed Allied victories, many of the military and civilians in Washington knew how serious the situation really was. The country was fighting a war on two fronts.

And the monetary cost was staggering. The President, in his "fireside chats" was calling for austerity at home. Many items of daily use were rationed. Such mundane things as toilet paper, paper towels, aluminum foil, toothpicks, hairpins, and silk stockings, were in short supply, if almost impossible to obtain.

Elizabeth had written Becka a very funny letter about using the Sears catalog for "sanitary purposes" in the bathroom. She wrote that gasoline, as well as sugar and coffee were rationed. "We can do without the sugar, and I guess, Ben can stand to drink less coffee," she wrote "but it's hard to do without the gasoline for the car!" Still, Ben and Elizabeth did little complaining about shortages feeling their small inconveniences were minor compared to what their boys were experiencing at the battlefront.

41494 FJ

UNITED STATES OF AMERICA
OFFICE OF PRICE ADMINISTRATION

WAR RATION BOOK FOUR

Issued to Sharon L Duncan
(Print first, middle, and last names)

Complete address 400 Bellefonte Rd
Ashland Ky

READ BEFORE SIGNING

In accepting this book, I recognize that it remains the property of the United States Government. I will use it only in the manner and for the purposes authorized by the Office of Price Administration.

Void if Altered .... OCT 5 1945
(Signature)

It is a criminal offense to violate rationing regulations.

OPA Form R-145 16—35570-1

Ration Booklet

Elizabeth organized "war bond" rallies, and on one occasion, when Becka was home for the weekend, Liz asked her to sing for a rally at the local high school gym. Hundreds of people attended the rally and many donations were made. Becka sang "Remember Pearl Harbor," "God Bless America" and just for fun, "Beer Barrel Polka." She received standing applause and sang other songs requested, such as "Cherry Blossom Time," "Moonlight Becomes You," and other songs popular at the time.

The rally would have been a total success if the sound system had worked properly. In the middle of Becka's "Beer Barrel Polka," the sound system started "singing" a tune all its own! Becka motioned for the operator to turn it off, then asked the audience to sing along. They did, and the "show went on."

When Becka returned to her job in Washington, she joined the USO and became a "stage door canteen hostess." It was fun and exciting. She met Bing Crosby, Nelson Eddie and Janette McDonald, and many more movie and stage actors. She and Edna joined an organization called "The Girl's Reserve." They had their pictures taken and wore a badge, and were taken by bus to nearby military camps for dances and picnics.

Becka's favorite place was the Annapolis Academy. Edna loved going, because her "boy friend" had graduated from there and told her so much about it. She told Becka that he was a little jealous when she went for dances at the Academy. He really didn't want her dancing with other guys. The two were getting serious, and Edna told Becka that they had talked of getting married, now, instead of waiting until the war was over.

"Great!" Becka said, "I'll be your maid of honor, and you can ask the pastor in the big Baptist Church here in Washington, to perform the ceremony."

"Hmm," mused Edna. "I'll see if that would be O.K. with Jack."

One morning about a week later, while Becka was sorting the mail for Commander Reynolds, she came across a letter from El Toro Marine Corps Air Station in California. The letter listed an opening for a secretary at the base. Becka remembered the dream she had had about the ocean. Could that have been California? Without mentioning the dream or her intentions to anyone, she took the information from the letter and applied for the job.

Meanwhile Edna and Jack had planned ahead for their wedding. The weather was cold and blustery in Washington, but planning went forward in spite of it. Many friends from their work as well as relatives from Oklahoma were invited and planned to attend. Becka helped with the planning arranging for flowers, food, drinks, the wedding cake, etc.

The wedding was set for 2 p.m. on Saturday. Edna looked lovely in a pale blue traveling suit, and the groom was handsome in his uniform. Becka could hardly believe that everything went smoothly "without a hitch" and the young couple were married and off on a short honeymoon. They wouldn't say where they were going, but Becka suspected they were going to upstate New York to a ski lodge. Both Edna and Jack loved to ski.

A week after the wedding, a letter came for Becka from the El Toro Marine Air Base in California. She had the job for which she had applied, and was to report for work by the 14th of February. (Her birthday!) Becka wrote to her family telling them of her plans to move to California. Ever since she was a little child she had thought of California, and especially the southern part of the state. She had read many stories about the area, and wanted to see it. Besides, she thought, California is a lot closer to Hawaii where Bill is stationed. Maybe, just maybe, she thought, he could get a leave to come to California to see her.

When she told Commander Reynolds about her plans, he told her that she would have to get a release from the Navy Dept. because in wartime civilian employees were "frozen" to their jobs, except for "family emergencies."

Hmm, thought Becka, what kind of "family emergency" would I need to take me to California? Fortunately, the head of the personnel department supplied the answer.

"I see that you have applied and been accepted for a job at the Marine Base in El Toro. Why do you wish to transfer there?" Before Becka could answer, the woman continued, "Do you have a family member there? Perhaps a future husband?"

"Yes," Becka said without hesitation. "My future husband."

She smiled at the woman interviewing her, and hoped fervently that the woman would not ask for "his" name or location. "I want to go there to be near him." Becka continued, still smiling.

The woman looked at Becka for a moment, then, with a smile of her own, stamped the letter for approval.

"Good luck" she said, extending her hand. "I hope all goes well with you. As you already know, you will be expected to pay for your own transportation to the west coast. And if I may suggest? Take the train…and get a sleeper car. It's a long trip out there."

Becka shook her hand with a smile saying that indeed, taking the train was a good idea. She thanked the woman and left the office. She was elated. Outside the wind was howling and it was "spitting" snow. As she stood at the curb waiting for the streetcar, she pulled her coat around her and put her mittened hands in her pockets.

Jeeze, she thought, it is colder here than Alaska during January. She closed her eyes and "dreamed" of warm sunshine and sandy beaches.

The next day Commander Reynolds came to Becka's desk and asked her to come into the conference room to "take a few notes." Becka got her pad and pencil and entered the conference room.

"Surprise!" came the voices of many of her friends and co-workers. "Surprise! We all wanted to wish you good luck!"

Her co-workers crowded around her asking her many questions, and telling her they would miss her very much. Becka's eyes were misty and she wiped a tear from her cheek. Commander Reynolds put an arm around her, and said, "I don't know how we'll get along with out you. You kept this place filled with excitement and fun. We never knew who you might spill coffee on next!" The room roared with laughter. Everyone remembered Becka's "encounter" with Admiral Nimitz. Becka spent the next few days helping the new girl learn her job. She was a girl from the typing pool and this would be a promotion for her.

Becka was truly fond of Commander Reynolds, and was sad to leave, but still anxious for this new adventure. She told Mrs. Johnson at the boarding house that she was leaving, and said goodbye to Gwennie and Betty Ann and her other friends who lived there. Edna and Jack had returned from their honeymoon, and had found an apartment on Biltmore Street. They were fortunate to find the place and were busy getting settled in.

Becka went to see them and told Edna of her intentions to move to California. Edna did not seem surprised. "You'll be a lot closer to Hawaii," she teased. "We hope you'll keep in touch." Both girls hugged and there were a few tears.

They loved each other as sisters. Then, on February 5th Becka took the train to Ashland to see her parents.

Ben and Elizabeth were not too happy to see Becka get a one-way ticket to California. "Why don't you get a round-trip? "Elizabeth asked, "Then if you don't like it you can come right back home."

"No Mom," Becka shook her head "I only have enough money for one-way," and before Elizabeth could protest further, Becka continued. "besides, I'll need money to rent a place, and get settled. My job there begins on the 14th."

Becka had figured her expenses to the last penny. She did not intend to take money from her parents, and had saved enough for the move. She had taken the advice of the woman in the personnel office and purchased a birth in a "sleeper coach" and planned to arrive at her destination a few days early. She wanted to find an apartment or room before she needed to report for work.

"Becka and friends, Laguna Beach"

"Military service"

*"Fighter Squadron,
Red 2nd from left."*

CHAPTER EIGHT

California and the West Coast, 1944

IT WAS mid-January, and for Becka, the train trip to California was interesting and exciting. The farthest she had ever traveled from home was to Washington, and parts of Virginia and West Virginia. And the day she left Ashland, the weather could not have been worse. It had been raining all night and the next morning the rain had turned to snow and sleet. The wind is coming from the North Pole, Becka thought.

She had to take the train from Ashland to Chicago in order to get connections to Los Angeles, and when she left Chicago, the weather was worse than in Kentucky…if that were possible. Sleet, snow, and icy wind chilling one to the bone! Becka wore her warmest outfit, a three-piece wool suit, overcoat, and fur lined boots and fur mittens. She had a warm, fur-lined Stetson hat that was mink brown with flaps that could be pulled down to cover the ears.

The train trip west was fun. Becka met other passengers and enjoyed card games with a young marine traveling west to visit his parents. He had a ten-day leave before he too had to report to El Toro Air Base.

They talked about the Base, and what each might expect when they arrived. Sgt. Ron Williams, the young Marine, told Becka that he was born in Santa Ana, Calif. and that his parents still lived there. He was being transferred to El Toro from Cherry Point, North Carolina. He was a "master mechanic," and, as he told Becka, he knew airplane engines.

The morning their train pulled into Pomona, Calif. Becka raised the curtain in the window of her birth and peeked out. What she saw, she said later, made her feel as though she'd "died and gone to Heaven!" Outside the window of the slow moving train were little children playing barefoot! And women...walking around in low-backed sun dresses...and bright sunshine...and orange trees...and flowers...flowers blooming everywhere.... in January!

Becka dressed quickly and immediately realized that her clothes were all wrong for this climate.

Hmm, she smiled, new wardrobe!

Quickly managing to get all her things together, Becka was ready and anxious when the train stopped in Los Angeles. She located a bus to take her to Laguna Beach, the closest town to the Air Base.

Being wartime, all the buses were packed, and she had to stand in the aisle, her luggage stored in a compartment under the bus. It was a jolting, uncomfortable ride, but Becka was used to this, having ridden the streetcars in Washington, and when she arrived in Laguna Beach, she found a locker to store her luggage.

An hour later she'd located a local newspaper, and now… heaven! She was sitting on a bench at the beach, with her feet in the sand and the sun on her face…in the middle of January!

She began looking for a place to live...nothing. But, she'd heard on the bus that the Laguna Beach postmaster was a post-mistress. Hmm, she thought, a postmistress would probably know about vacancies.

Memories of snow, sleet, and howling wind made the sunny day and warm sand of Laguna Beach feel wonderful, but right now she had more urgent business. Becka walked to the Post Office and as she entered, she asked to speak to the Postmistress.

"Hello" said Becka as she was introduced to Mrs. Knight. "I just got into town and I'm looking for a place to stay. I thought maybe you could help me?"

"Do you have family here?" Mrs. Knight asked Becka.

"No, I don't know anyone. You see, I have a job at the Marine Air Base, and have to report for work on the 14th, my birthday," and Becka smiled her most charming smile.

Mrs. Knight decided that she liked this pretty young woman. Yes, she thought, I'll try to help her find a place. "Well, I do know a Navy Chief and his wife who live here in Laguna Beach. They have an apartment over their garage that has just been vacated." She smiled at Becka. "I'll just give them a call. Maybe it hasn't been rented yet."

Becka said a silent prayer that she would be able to rent the apartment. She loved Laguna Beach already, and had a feeling that she would really enjoy living here. The Postmistress turned and told Becka that the apartment was available. Becka's prayer was answered.

She thanked Mrs. Knight, and promising to keep in touch, quickly left to find her things that were stored in the bus station locker. She got a cab and was soon at her destination, Through Street, a small street about a half mile from the downtown area of Laguna Beach.

She met the young couple that lived in the house and was shown the apartment over the attached garage. It was absolutely charming and ideal for Becka. The apartment had a living-sleeping area, a tiny kitchen, and a bath with a little dressing room and walk-in closet. There was a small fenced yard in the back full of flowers—roses, geraniums, bougainvillea and oleander—and everything was in bloom.... in February! Delighted, Becka could hardly believe her luck, and best of all it was only fifty dollars a month!

From there she surveyed the surrounding neighborhood. How different it is from home, she thought. To the East were beautiful mountains covered with short trees called the "Elfin Forest." To the south lay the city and residential neighborhoods, houses painted pink, pale blue, and mint green, and flowers blooming everywhere. To the West she could see a portion of the mighty Pacific Ocean, as blue as the sky above.

This has to be the most beautiful little city in the whole country, Becka thought. She felt a joy in her heart she had not felt for a long time.

She went inside and looked around. The furniture is nice, she thought. With a few colorful pillows and some new curtains, new tea towels, and vases of flowers, it will be a lovely place to live. She needed to go to the grocery store for milk, bread and other necessities, but everything was so close she could walk to the stores with little trouble.

But first, she thought, I'll go for a walk on the beach while it's still daylight.

Grabbing a sweater—which I probably won't even

need— she walked down the street and across the way to the beach. It was warm and the sun was low in the western sky with a slight breeze blowing off the ocean. She stooped down and took off her shoes and socks, tied the laces together and hung them around her neck. Tying her sweater around her waist, she set off up the beach.

The water was cold to her bare feet but the sand was warm, the waves lapping over her toes as she walked. Seabirds whirled and called overhead; the breeze tasted salty as it kissed her face and ruffled her long thick hair.

Becka felt very alive and happy. She noticed others as they strolled the beach, threw balls to their children, or just sat on blankets on the sand. There were not many folks on the beach…not at all like Virginia Beach where she had spent a weekend with some of her girlfriends two summers ago. Gosh, she remembered, what a sunburn I got that weekend!

Right after the 4th of July, she and Edna, Betty Ann, and Gwennie had planned the trip for the weekend. Becka had a cousin living near Virginia Beach who had invited the girls to stay over Saturday night, so they'd taken a boat from Washington down the Chesapeake Bay, then on to Virginia Beach.

Of course, they'd had little exposure to the sun up to that time, working every day and doing other things on the weekends – shows, dances, parties, etc. Nevertheless, the girls purchased lovely new bathing suits, beach towels, and swim caps, and brought along inflatable beach toys. But not much suntan oil…they all wanted to "get a real tan."

Well, Becka remembered, we all got a "real tan" all right.

The day at the beach had been overcast, with little or no sun and they were all disappointed, but decided to make the most of the day, anyway. Spreading out their towels, they donned their swim caps, and along with the inflated swim rings, entered the waves. The water was warm and inviting, the surf was not too high, and they enjoyed their frolic in the Atlantic.

Returning to the beach they stretched out on the sand, without applying any suntan oil, and began to "get a tan."

Oooh boy, what a tan!! She grimaced.

The ultra violet rays of the sun had "kissed" their lily-white legs, arms, backs and faces. In fact, there was (practically) not a spot on their bodies that wouldn't be "kissed," and later they would find a sharp contrast to the still lily white skin that had been protected by their skimpy bathing suits.

But at the time they hadn't realize just how burned they were—not until they'd taken their showers. And, they'd been warned. Becka's cousin had told them before they went out that they could get bad sunburns on a cloudy day. But somehow they had forgotten her warning. She "doctored" the girls with lotions and creams, but all four were miserable. They'd slept little that night, and the boat ride back to Washington was "a nightmare!"

Now as Becka walked along the sandy beach in Laguna, she smiled at the memory…but wouldn't make that mistake again. She also remembered she'd had a fever and chills, and a hard time working on the Monday after the weekend trip. They were not permitted to take "sick leave" for anything so trivial as sunburn, but Bill had taken pity on them and allowed the girls to go home early.

Thinking of those days brought the memory of Bill to Becka's mind. She wondered where he was now. Was he still in Hawaii? Had he been sent into combat? She had not heard from him since she had written to him that she was transferring to El Toro. She must send him her new address right away.

She found a large beach stone and sat down. The sun was dipping low in the western sky. Long streaks of pink, orange and yellow painted the sky lovely hues. The sun on the water traced a silvery path across the Pacific right up to the foaming waves coming onto the beach and licking close to where Becka sat. How lovely this is, she thought. It's so warm.... and in February! It was hard for her to believe.

Becka strolled back down the beach. She was in no hurry, enjoying herself, and relishing her new surroundings. Finally, though, she brushed the sand from her feet, put on her shoes, and feeling a little chilly for the first time, put on her sweater. Stopping at a corner store, she bought milk, cereal and bread, lunchmeat, and other necessities. She walked up the hill to her apartment, fixed herself a sandwich, drank some milk and prepared for bed.

It was too late to call her parents in Kentucky. They would be in bed by this time, she thought. As she climbed into her "new" bed, she said a prayer of thanks for her new place and her good fortune in finding it. She prayed that her new position at El Toro would be something interesting and even worthwhile. She, like Bill, had never felt that the work she did in Washington was meaningful. Especially the first six months while she was working the afternoon shift.

Becka, like her parents, had a "sense of patriotism." She regularly bought war bonds, and kept abreast of what was happening on the front lines of battle. With Harry on a ship out in the Pacific, and Henry on the front lines in France, she had great interest in the progress of the war on both fronts. Her letters from them were scant, and sometimes she would receive several all at once, then go for weeks without hearing. Now, because of the move to the West Coast, her mail would probably be delayed even further.

That night Becka had one of her "dreams." It was the same dream she had had several times before. She was walking along the beach, listening to the pounding waves and the sea birds...she was happy...she was meeting someone...but she could not see who it was—fog and mist shrouded the identity.

Still, she was happy and woke up feeling excited and eager for her day. On her first day of work, Becka took the small bus that ran from Laguna Beach to El Toro Air Base. She found that the work there was similar to the work she had done for Commander Reynolds in Washington: exacting and demanding. She welcomed it. From her desk she could see out across the airfield and get glimpses of the fighter planes as they took off and landed. She brought her lunch and sat with other workers in a shady area, equipped with picnic tables.

Becka quickly became acquainted with some of the other office workers, and enjoyed their stories of life in and around an active Fightert Base. All of the employees, both military and civilian, kept up with the "war news." Becka was especially interested in news of the European front, and the progress of the Navy Fleet in the Pacific. She had sent both her parents and her brothers and sister her new address in Laguna Beach, however, she had only heard from her parents and her sister Maggie. She knew it was early to hear from Harry or Henry. Still, she was anxious to know how they were doing.

She had lived here in Laguna Beach for several weeks now, and liked it better all the time, but those first few weeks were an adjustment for her in many ways. First, she didn't have the right clothes. Everything seemed to be too heavy—certainly not in "California beach style." Second, she had an adjustment with the drastic difference in the weather, although this was an easy adjustment! It was March, and the weather felt like June!

She wore a size seven and found many cute outfits in her size. It was certainly fun to shop, and clothes were actually less expensive than in the Capital. And she had met some interesting young men in uniform. One of them, Curly Adams, (a young flyer nicknamed "Curly" because of his curly brown hair) had asked her for a date.

She agreed to see him on Saturday, for lunch and a walk on the beach. When he arrived at her little apartment, she had lunch ready and suggested that they climb to the top of the "hill" in back of her apartment and have lunch when they reached the top. She had fried chicken, fruit and drinks in a small easy-to-carry container.

"Isn't that a beautiful hill?" she asked Curly as they started out on their climb." It looks so pretty, all covered with those nice soft green bushes."

"I don't think those bushes will be easy to navigate," observed Curly. "That's chaparral, and it can be prickly and make walking difficult, and I'm afraid those bushes are far from soft, but we'll give it a try," he laughed, and started up the hill, holding Becka's hand and picking his way between the larges chaparral bushes.

They soon found out just how prickly those bushes could be! Before long they were exhausted and full of brambles and scratches. They didn't give up, however, and finally reached the top of the hill. There was an open area at the top, with a picnic table and palm branch umbrella. The two exhausted hikers gratefully sat down on the benches. As Becka was laying out their lunch, a tall leggy girl clad in shorts and a halter and wearing hiking shoes came swinging into the area. She looked fresh as a daisy, no brambles on her clothes, and no scratches on those long slim legs.

"Hi" she said, smiling at the two obviously exhausted "hikers."

"Hi," responded a surprised Becka. "How in the world did you make it up that hill without a scratch?"

"I just followed the trail up," she laughed. "Didn't you know there's a trail all the way up here?"

Becka and Curly just looked at each other, then shook their heads and laughed.

They ate their lunches and enjoyed the fantastic view from the top, a panoramic view of the city, mountains and ocean. Below them to the west lay the small city of Laguna Beach with its quaint homes and shops, the sandy beach curved around the city like a golden necklace. The hills to the south hugged the city and added a belt of green foliage, palm trees, live oaks, eucalyptus trees, and everywhere, orange and lemon trees.

The view was breathtakingly beautiful and Becka pulled her camera out of her pack and began to take pictures. A short time later they took the path back down the hill, walking slowly and enjoying themselves. When they reached the end of the trail, they found it was not far from the spot where they had started their climb!

"How on earth did we miss this trail?" Becka wondered.

"Well, I don't know either," said Curly. "Guess we haven't lived here long enough to know about a lot of things!"

Becka had already learned one thing: Laguna Beach was a Mecca for artists. There were many art galleries, art studios and many places to purchase art supplies. Becka wrote to Harry about the abundance of artists. She hoped that he could come here sometime. Harry would really appreciate a place like this.

Curly and Becka made a date to meet later that evening for dinner. Becka showered and "doctored" the scratches on her arms and legs. She put on a pale yellow pantsuit she had purchased at an exclusive little shop in Laguna Beach. It had a bolero jacket, embroidered in gold braid; the pants were cut well with slash pockets. She wore a long sleeved blouse of soft pale green satin.

"Wow" said Curly as he surveyed Becka that evening, "You look absolutely beautiful!"

"Why thank you," Becka answered smiling. "You look mighty handsome, yourself. That uniform and those wings on your tunic are impressive!"

"Well, come on gal," he said with a smile, "Let's go knock 'em dead!"

They climbed into Curly's small car and drove down to the center of the little city, where several restaurants lined the main street.

"Let's eat here," said Curly, stopping in front of a small restaurant, "I've heard they have a great steak."

They entered the restaurant and were shown to a large booth. The place smelled of steak and onions and Becka's mouth watered. Mmm, she thought, it sure smells good in here! After checking the menu, they ordered top sirloin steaks, baked potatoes, and a tossed green salad. Becka had iced tea and Curly had a beer.

They were enjoying the meal when Curly looked out the front window and saw a couple of his "flyer buddies." The two men outside looked in and saw Curly. He motioned for his friends to come in and join them. The booth was large and curved around so that the two men had not seen Becka from the window. When they walked in and around to the front of the booth they were surprised, and pleased, to see her.

"Hey, I'd like you to meet Becka," said Curly, as the men crowded into the booth. "Becka Young, this is Tex George, and Red Duncan."

The men smiled and each shook Becka's hand, but Red held on to her hand a little longer than was necessary and Becka felt a distinct current pass between them. Smiling a bit tentatively, she looked closely at Red.

"Those steaks look good. Do you mind if we order our own and join you?" he asked, looking steadily at Becka.

The two men ordered steaks with French fries and were soon eating with gusto.

"They sure serve a great steak here, don't you agree?" remarked Curly.

"Yeah, you can really pick 'em." grinned Red, looking at Becka with appreciation.

Yeah, thought Red, ol' Curly can really pick 'em. And knowing Curly's reputation as a 'womanizer' he wondered just how far Curly had "advanced" his relationship with this cute little girl.

"How long you two know each other?" he asked, still looking at Becka.

"Oh, we haven't known each other long." Becka answered. "We see each other at work, sometimes. And this morning we took a hike up the hill behind my apartment."

She looked at Curly, and they both began to laugh. They explained the difficult hike, and finding the trail after the fact. Tex was watching the interplay between Becka and Red, and was aware that Curly had not failed to notice Red's interest in "his" date.

"Say, Curly, we gotta leave," said Red. "I'm having some friends up to my room for drinks this evening. Why don't you bring Becka and come on up for a night cap?"

"Sure" answered Curly. "Would you like to go, Becka?" Becka looked at Red and nodded.

Yes, she thought, I'd definitely like to get to know these two men a little better.

Both men were very good looking. Red was over six feet four inches tall, broad shouldered and fair, with wavy reddish hair and very blue eyes. He had a great smile that showed even white teeth. Tex was a little shorter, and huskier built, with warm brown eyes and dark brown curcly hair. He had a long jagged scar that ran from his hairline on his left temple to the base of his jaw. He also had a decidedly Texas accent.

Becka found both men interesting and charming.

The two officers left after getting a promise from Curly to come over to the B.O.Q. to Red's room for a nightcap. Becka had never been in the Laguna Hotel where the Officer's quarters were located and looked around with interest when they entered the lobby. There were a few officers and some young women in the lobby and no one seemed to notice as she and Curly got on the elevator. Getting off at the 2nd floor, they walked down the hall to Red's room.

When she and Curly entered the room the "party" seemed to consist of Red, Tex, and one other officer. Red introduced Becka to his roommate, Captain "Ringer" Winters. Capt Winters looked Becka up and down in a very unflattering manner. Becka felt like he was "undressing" her with his eyes. It made her blush, and because she blushed she felt angry.

Feeling decidedly out of place she turned to Curly. "Come on, there's no party here, let's go."

"Oh," Ringer spoke up with a leer in his voice, "we can have a real party if that's what you want, little girl,"

Red turned quickly to Ringer. "Hey, lay off, will you?" Then turning his attention back to Becka and Curly. "Don't pay any attention to Ringer, he's three sheets to the wind."

All the men laughed, but Becka did not. Red looked at

Becka "I apologize for that Becka, please do stay, at least have one drink before you go." Then he whispered to Becka, "Ringer has just had a little too much to drink, he's really a prince of a guy."

Becka looked over at Ringer, who had gone back to lounging on the bed. He acts like he thinks he's "God's gift to women," she thought.

Becka turned to Curly, "I'm sorry, but I don't like this whole situation. I don't think I should be here. Why don't you take me home, then you can come back for your night-cap." A statement rather than a question, Becka turned walked to the door.

"Aw, Becka," Curly responded, "these guys are harmless, really. Let's stay for just one drink," he said, giving her a hug, "then I'll take you home, O.K.?"

Becka hesitated. Maybe she was being a little prudish. "Well, alright," she answered, managing a smile, "but just for a little while."

"That's our girl," said Red, handing Curly a large whisky and soda. "Now what's your pleasure, Becka?" Red turned to Becka with a most charming smile.

"Just a seven-up, please." She looked steadily at Red. Was he a little "drunk" too? She wondered. His face was flushed and his hands shook slightly. When he handed her the drink, she sipped it gingerly to make sure it was only a soft drink. It was. She found a chair by the door and sat down drinking her soda.

The men began to laugh and talk about their experiences flying and soon Curly was holding a fresh drink in his hand. Red had supplied Curly with three large drinks before she was able to convince him it was time to take her home.

"If you want to stay," she said, "I can walk home, it's not far, you know."

But Curly wouldn't hear of it, and graciously escorted her out the door after thanking Red for the drinks.

Becka learned much later that Red had been called on the carpet for having a girl in his room. There was a strict order against this, Red knew it, but decided to take his chances. He knew the C.O. and was not worried. The two men had a good laugh, and he was dismissed, "with a warning."

The drive up the hill to the apartment was only about three blocks, however, on the way Curly became violently ill, and had to pull over and throw up on the side of the street! Becka sat quietly beside him for a while to make sure he was all right. Curly looked at her with a sick expression on his face.

"I'm sorry, Becka. Those drinks Red gave me must have been 'fifty-fifties.' I don't know when I've ever had drinks hit me this hard!"

He looked positively "green around the gills." Becka felt sorry for him and assured him she could walk on home by herself.

"No, please" he said weakly, "I'll be alright in a few minutes." She nodded and waited, and in a few more minutes he started the car and drove her home. He apologized again and she got out and went alone up to her apartment.

As Becka was preparing for bed, her thoughts were whirling. I think Red deliberately got Curly drunk, she thought. Why? Why did he do that? I just don't understand it. They seemed to be friends. But I just don't like that Ringer. He is about the most conceited man I've met in a long time. I do like Red and Tex, but that was a dirty trick to play on poor Curly!

She drifted off to sleep thinking about all the things that had happened that day. It was March 19th, a day she would never forget.

The following Sunday, she joined the Navy Chief and his wife and attended a small chapel nearby. The church was crowded, but she did not see any of the men she had met the night before. She smiled to herself thinking they all probably had monumental hangovers this morning!

"Hello, Becka," said a sweet voice behind her.

Becka turned around and saw her friend, Mrs. Knight, the Postmistress. Becka smiled and shook her hand.

"Hi," she answered. "It's so nice to see you. Do you attend this church all the time?"

"Yes" Mrs. Knight replied.

Because it was such a pleasant day, Becka said she wanted to walk on the beach for a while, and would be home later. She left her friends and walked the few blocks to the beach. As she had done the first time she walked on the beach, she took off her shoes and socks and hung them around her neck. The sand felt warm and wonderful to her feet. The waves licked over her toes and ankles and the soft ocean breeze tasted salty on her lips. The seabirds, ever present, called and swirled above her head. Becka felt so alive and happy.

Suddenly she remembered her dream! She was going to meet someone! Only this was not a dream, she really was going to meet someone! Who? Becka strained to see far down the beach. There were many people on the seashore, but not one of them was "right."

A long distance away, she saw a man walking toward her. He was in uniform. He was barefoot, with his shoes hanging around his neck. She could not see his face. As he drew nearer, a heavy fog and mist obscured her vision. Was she still dreaming? Will I ever be able to see who is hidden in the mist? She thought. Suddenly someone was close beside her. She felt his presence first, and then he spoke.

"Hello, Becka" said a voice she well remembered, "I've been looking for you. They told me up at your house that you were somewhere down on the beach."

Becka turned, and through the mist saw "Red" Clark Duncan! Red reached down and took both of her hands. "Come on" he said, "Let's walk. The fog is lifting. It should be a beautiful sunset."

"Red"

"Becka"

CHAPTER NINE

Becka and Red – 1944

THEY FOUND one of the many benches located along the sandy shore. Sitting down, they watched the sun slowly sinking into the western sky. It was March, and the days were short. The gulls swirled overhead, calling and chattering. The waves broke on the beach leaving long curls of lacy foam. Peeking under the low hanging fog bank, the sun sent streaks of yellow and orange across the waters. The crest of the waves sparkled like a million diamonds.

"It is so beautiful." Becka said in a soft voice.

"It's beautiful because we are here together," Red said and squeezed Becka's hand. He leaned down and kissed her parted lips, tasting the sweetness of her mingled with the salty taste of the sea. As their lips touched they felt the current they had felt the first time their hands had touched the night they met. Red pulled her closer and deepened the kiss. His heart was pounding and he felt a great desire filling him. After a moment Becka pulled away.

"Please," she whispered, somewhat out of breath. "We're in public, you know." She laughed, a little nervously.

Damn, thought Red, I'm rushing this. If I'm not careful I'll scare her away. "You're right, Becka, I'm sorry." He did not remove his arm from around her, though.

"You are just so darn sweet!" Becka pulled away, stooped down to brush the sand from her feet, and started to replace her shoes and socks. Red did the same, and they were soon walking back on the boardwalk toward Red's car, a beautiful little 1941 Ford.

"Can I give you a lift home?" Red asked.

"No," said Becka, reluctantly, "I think I'd rather walk home, it's only a few blocks. But thanks."

"Then…may I take you to dinner tonight? It's early yet, and we both have to eat."

"Sure," Becka said, nodding. "But I can't be ready until about eight."

Red looked at her admiringly. "Don't change," he said in that Texas drawl, "You look absolutely beautiful the way you are."

"Thank you," Becka said, smiling.

Becka left him and walked the three blocks up to her apartment. She needed the time to clear her head. Whoa, she thought, what's happening here?

Her thoughts turned to Bill, in Hawaii, or perhaps he was out to sea on a battleship. She hadn't heard from him in weeks. She thought of Curly, how did she feel about him? But she could not get Red out of her mind.

When she reached her apartment and climbed the stairs, many thoughts swirled in her head. She found the key and entered her little home. It invited her, with pretty colorful pillows, matching curtains and tea towels. Her books and magazines were scattered across the small coffee table. The teapot waited in the tiny kitchen. The fragrance of roses from her small yard filled the air.

She looked at her watch. It was past seven; she must get a move on. He'll probably be on time, and I don't want to keep him waiting. She quickly bathed and dressed, selecting a soft floral dress that clung to her small body in a most appealing manner. She brushed her long thick hair until it shone. Needing little make-up, she applied a small amount of lip-gloss. A touch of her favorite perfume and she was ready.

As she reached for a beautifully crocheted white shawl that had been made by her mother, she heard steps on the stairs. The doorbell sounded and Becka went to open the door. To her surprise, Red was not alone. Tex was with him!

"Hi, Becka," said Tex before she could voice her surprise. "I hope you don't mind if I tag along? You see," he went on hurriedly, "Well, you see I went over to Red's room to see if he had your, umm, telephone number. He said he was coming up here to take you to dinner. And I'll be danged if he didn't ask me if I wanted to come. So here I am."

He grinned at Becka and Red, and all three began to laugh.

Wow, thought Becka, I'll probably be the envy of all the gals in town, when they see me escorted by two handsome flyers.

And the men were handsome! Red was so tall, with his thick reddish blond hair that curled across his head. And his green flier's uniform fit him perfectly. He had a row of medals across his chest, and the flyers' wings looked impressive on his tunic.

Tex was a little shorter, but his soft brown eyes twinkled when he laughed, and his stocky build filled out his uniform very nicely. The long scar on the left side of his face only added to his rugged good looks. To say that she was pleased to be with them would be an understatement! As the three climbed into Red's blue Ford, Tex sat in the back seat.

"We should take my car," Tex said, "it's much purtier and a lot more cozy!"

"Yeah, Tex, you're right," said Red with amusement. "You see Becka, Tex has a red convertible, and you're lucky if you can squeeze two people in it."

Tex leaned over the front seat and whispered in Becka's ear, "Don't pay him no never mind, little lady. Just you wait 'till I take you for a joy ride in my little red buggy!"

Becka laughed and turned toward Tex. His face was so close to hers that she thought he was going to kiss her.

"Hey, Tex" said Red "lay off, or you'll be walking home!"
"O.K." laughed Tex, "just kidding."

Only I'm not kidding, thought Tex. I'd like to take this little gal out. And if Red's not serious about her, I will.

They drove down to the main part of town and stopped at the same "White House" restaurant where they had all met. "This place has really good steaks, don't you agree, Becka?" Red turned to Becka with a smile.

"Uh huh," she nodded.

The three found a large circular booth and ordered dinner. They were served a tossed green salad and drinks before dinner, and a wooden bowl held a napkin-wrapped loaf of warm bread.

The fragrance of the bread made all three hungry, but when the steaks arrived, to Becka's disappointment her steak was tough. She didn't say anything, but proceeded to eat it as best she could. As she was cutting off a particularly tough piece, her knife slipped and a portion of the steak, along with the French fries, flew across the table as though jet-propelled and landed, in full glory, in Tex's lap!

If the floor could have opened up and swallowed Becka at that moment, she would have been eternally grateful! There was stunned silence for a few seconds, then Tex reached down into his lap and picked up a limp, catsup covered French fry and leaned forward, looking around Becka. Shaking the French fry back and forth, he said to Red "She's with you, ain't she Dunc?" Red shook his head, "No Tex, she's with YOU!"

Both men roared with laughter as Becka's face turned bright red. She tried to laugh, but could only think that she would probably never see either of these gorgeous men again! A waiter arrived quickly and cleaned up the mess, leaving only a few catsup stains, but Becka could only cover her face with her hands.

Both men put their arms around her. "You're not crying are you?" asked Red, still smiling.

Becka was able to compose herself, and managed to laugh with the men.

It was funny, I guess, she thought. But I've probably ruined my chances with my klutzy behavior. They won't want anything to do with such a "boob."

But, happily she was wrong. When Red and Tex took her home that evening, Red asked if he could call her the next day.

"Hey," said Tex, "I was going to ask you the same thing!"

"Too bad, old buddy, I just beat you to it," said Red.

That following weekend, Red arrived at Becka's apartment early. He had called and said he wanted to pick Becka up before nine a.m. He said he "had a surprise" for her. Becka loved surprises. He had told her to dress "comfortably, and wear comfortable shoes." She had a Levi outfit and walking shoes on when he arrived.

"You look great!" Red said as he surveyed her outfit.

He was wearing his khaki uniform and looked very handsome to Becka. However, she just smiled and thanked him, then asked, "What is the surprise?"

Red laughed and said "Grab your purse and come on, I'll tell you on the way."

The two climbed into the little blue Ford and Red drove down the coast, out of the city. They were soon traveling along the coast highway south toward San Diego.

Becka had not been out of the city except for the bus ride to El Toro, and she was thrilled to see the countryside. Groves of orange trees lined the sides of the highway, and the rolling hills to the east were beautiful. The long expanse of the Pacific stretched beyond them to the west. The weather was warm and breezy, and Becka had the window of the car open in order to catch the breeze and to smell the fragrance of the orange blossoms.

"Oh Red!" Becka cried, "Can we please stop for a few minutes? I've never picked an orange off an orange tree!"

"Sure," answered Red "But I'll need to drive down one of these little grove roads first, we can't stop here on the main highway."

Red maneuvered the little blue Ford down a dirt road located in one of the large groves of orange trees. He stopped the car, and Becka jumped out and ran to the nearest tree. She reached up and pulled a large, very ripe orange off the nearest branch.

"Come on, Red, you pick one too!" she said excitedly.

"O.K." Red said, and pulled a nice fat orange off another branch.

"Let's get out of here," Red said laughing. "We're breaking the law, you know."

They both climbed back into the car and Red backed down the little dirt road to the highway. They parked off the road a little way down the highway and peeled and ate the oranges. They were sweet and juicy. Becka had Kleenexes in her purse, and they laughed and wiped the juice off their faces.

Red looked at Becka's happy face. Hells bells, he thought, I think I'm really falling for this sweet little girl. He reached over and pulled Becka into his arms and kissed her. Her lips were soft and inviting, and she did not pull away, but returned his kiss. Presently, Red started the car and they continued down the highway toward San Diego. As they drove along Becka enjoyed the view of the Pacific Ocean, the beaches and the ever-present gulls. She looked at Red with a bright smile.

"You are so much fun to be with, do you know that?" he whispered into her hair.

He stopped the car at a small overlook area, then pulled the hair off her soft neck and kissed her ear, her cheek, and then he found her mouth again.

Becka gently pushed him away. "We'd better get going, I still haven't seen that surprise you promised me."

Red laughed and started the car. They pulled back onto the highway and continued toward the San Diego area. The countryside around San Diego was beautiful. They drove along the bay and admired the view of the sea, the rolling hills the palm trees, and the bougainvillea. There were birds everywhere.

"This has to be the most beautiful place I've ever seen," remarked Becka.

"Yeah," drawled Red. "It is beautiful around these parts. But the South Pacific islands are sure pretty, too. Or they would be great if there wasn't a war going on to spoil it," he amended.

"Can you tell me a little of your experiences while you were out there?" asked Becka. She was very curious about his ribbons and his war record. But she also knew that many of the guys returning from active duty were reluctant to talk about it. Red waited a few moments, and then he glanced over at Becka.

"You really want to know?" he asked softly.

"Yes, I do, " said Becka, "If you want to tell me."

"Well," drawled Red "It's a hell of a war. I'm damn lucky to be up in the air and not down there on the ground. All that jungle, heat, flies, mosquitoes; slugging it out in hand-to-hand combat, believe me, we "fly boys" have it damn easy compared to our ground war buddies. You know, Becka, I really don't see, up close, the damage I do when I strafe an area. Nor do I see the loss of life I inflict on the enemy when I release my bombs." Red paused.

Becka remained silent listening, and wondering, as she pictured the planes, the smoke and the destruction. Some of the aspects of the vivid dreams she had had recently came to her mind. She shuddered involuntarily. Red noticed her reaction.

"Aw, honey, let's not talk about it today. We're on a good time jaunt and talking about the war will spoil my surprise."

Becka leaned over and put her hand on Red's arm. "O.K." she said, "You can tell me later." She smiled at him. "What's that ahead?" she asked. She had not been reading the roadside signs and had not noticed that they were approaching the Mexican border.

"Well, my sweet, here we are at the surprise I promised you." Red pulled up to the border crossing. The Mexican guards waved them on through the crossing, and they proceeded along a rough and unpaved road.

Becka saw immediately the poverty and unkempt condition of the roads and buildings. There were many shacks and tumbled down houses clinging to the hillsides. Dirty, hungry looking children were everywhere, mangy looking dogs roamed the streets, and there was the smell of raw sewage mingled with cooking odors. It reminded Becka of some of the slum areas she had seen in Washington, D.C. when she was working there.

Often the streetcars traveled through areas of that great city that were dangerous. In these parts of the city, she knew, she was lucky to be on the streetcar, sitting up near the driver. Now as she and Red drove through this place, she truly felt "a foreigner" and instinctively moved closer to Red, looking at him uneasily.

"Don't be nervous, honey," Red said, noticing her uneasiness. "It's all right. We are safe here, honest."

Presently they were driving down a broad street, much smoother and with many more cars and people around. Red found a parking place in front of a nice looking store. He got out and walked around to her side of the car and opened the door for her.

"Come on, Sweetie," he grinned. "I'm about to show you the surprise I promised you."

Becka took his offered hand and the two walked together into the store. Becka looked around. The store was neat and clean, with many colorful shawls, costume jewelry, lovely pottery and unusual handmade items on all the counters. A nice looking elderly man with a grey beard and grey hair approached them with a wide smile.

"Buenos Dias!" he said, as they approached. Then, "Good morning, Senior. May I show you something for the beautiful lady?" He glanced quickly from Red to Becka.

"Buenos Dias, Senor" answered Red, returning the gentleman's smile. "Just let us look around for a few minutes. When we find something we want, we'll call you."

Becka was fascinated with everything she saw. Red bought her one of the lovely shawls, a hand tooled, leather pocket book, several pairs of silk stockings, and a lovely hand made ceramic duck. It was delicately painted and very charming.

When they were back in the car and traveling again toward the border crossing, Red told her that all the things he had purchased did not even total ten dollars in U.S. Money!

"Thanks, Red," Becka said, smiling at him. "This has been a wonderful surprise! Where were you born, Red? I know so little about you. You seem to know Spanish, because you spoke to the clerk so well. I know a little high school Spanish, but I'm afraid I'd be lost if I tried to negotiate any business down here."

As they drove North after crossing over into the U.S., Red began to tell Becka something about his life growing up in West Texas.

"I was born in Lawton, Oklahoma. My father died when I was very young. My mother had to work so I went to Midland, Texas, to live with my grandmother." Red shrugged. "She was more like my mother than my grandmother to me. We lived outside Midland on a dairy farm, and had about 60 cows that had to be milked twice a day. But we didn't process the milk. We'd put it in large milk cans and haul it into Midland where it'd be processed, bottled and sold." He grinned at her and laughed, then held up his hand for Becka's inspection. "See here? You can tell by the knuckles on my fingers that I've milked a few cows in my day. When I was only seven years old," he went on, "I was taught to drive the truck. It was only while some of the men threw bales of hay out for the cattle, but I was large and tall for my age. It was still a stretch to reach the pedals of that truck, though!

"By the time I was twelve I was really driving that truck — driving it into town to deliver the milk. After deliveries I'd drive back to the farm, change clothes, and ride my pony back to school.

"I used to get in trouble a lot for being late to school, too. That damn pony was hard to manage and if we were traveling along beside the railroad track, that stubborn son-of-a-gun would try to keep up with the passing trains, no matter in what direction the train was going, east or west. It didn't matter to him. And, of course, he'd take me along with him!"

As Red laughed at the memory, Becka pictured a small redheaded, freckled faced boy trying to control a stubborn pony as they raced a passing train.

"My high school days were pretty grim." He went on. "We lived seven miles out of the city. It was too far to drive if I had a date. My social life consisted of hitching a ride into town and going to a movie and having a coke afterwards. In the summertime, I talked my grandmother into putting my bed outside under a tree, and that's where I slept. When it looked like rain I pulled the bed into the milk room and slept in there. I had to examine my bed before I climbed into it. There were rattlesnakes on the farm!

"There weren't many other youngsters for me to play with, so I made my own fun. My Uncle gave me a 22 rifle when I was about 12 years old, and believe me, all small squirrels, jackrabbits and rattlesnakes were not safe when that little red-headed kid was around!"

Red continued as Becka listened quietly. "There was a boy about my age living on a nearby ranch. They owned half the county, probably ten thousand acres, and were very wealthy. He would ride his horse up to our property, climb over our fence and go hunting with me.

We had a lot of fun together in the summer, but he was sent off to a private school during the winter. We've kept in touch with each other over the years, though. He went to West Point and now he's in the army...somewhere in France. . I haven't heard from him for a while now. I hope he's O.K."

Red looked at Becka and seeing that she was really interested in what he was saying, he continued. "When I finished high school, I moved to Illinois and attended the University there. I lived with my mother's sister. My mom had remarried to a very nice guy, but I never lived with them. When the war broke out I had already enlisted in the Navy...Navy first for training, then I transferred to the Marine Fighters. And there, my sweet Becka, is basically the story of my life."

Red had pulled the car into a gas station, and the two were drinking a soft drink as he had continued to tell her about himself.

"Is your grandmother still alive?" asked Becka,

"Yes, she is," said Red. "She still lives near Midland, with a cousin. We keep in touch."

After filling the tank, Red pulled the car back on the highway, and they continued on North toward Laguna Beach. Red had told Becka earlier that he had special "chits" for gas, as there was a real shortage because of the war.

"Hey, little dolly, how about you? Do you have a large family?"

"Yes, I guess you would say so. I have three brothers and one sister. My parents are alive and well and living in the same house where I was born." Becka told Red about her brothers, Harry and Henry, and Will, and her sister Maggie.

"My brothers Harry and Henry are both in the service. Henry is a war correspondent and stationed in Europe. He is near the front lines. Harry is an officer in the Navy and is on a battleship in the Pacific. My oldest brother Will is a civilian employee at the shipyards on the East coast. He's married with two little girls. Maggie is married to an army sergeant and living near Joplin, Mo."

Becka looked at Red and smiled. He listened quietly as she talked, keeping his eyes on the road, but glancing often at Becka. "You know," said Red quietly, "I envy you that big family. I never really had a family. I always felt misplaced, somehow. Not really belonging, I guess."

"You didn't feel as though your grandmother was your family?" Becka asked.

"Well, not really. It was just Memo and her husband—who was not my grandfather—he was her third husband. I don't think he liked me very much. Oh, we got on O.K., but there was just that feeling."

Red rubbed his chin and scratched his eyebrow. He had a habit of doing that when he was thinking, Becka thought as she watched him. They drove on quietly, both wrapped in their own thoughts. Becka's heart felt the pain of that little redheaded kid on the big farm in Texas. She could feel his loneliness and his longing for a brother or sister. Perhaps he had felt a deep desire to be with his mother, but was unable to express his feelings.

Talking about his childhood brought memories back to Red that he would probably rather forget. He had managed to put most of the painful memories behind him, and chose to recall the brighter moments.

"What were your favorite classes in high school?" Becka asked.

"Oh, I liked math and science, but my favorite school experience was playing the big bass drum in the marching band. I was also the baton twirler when they needed one." Red laughed at the memory. "I never was able to participate in sports because I had so much work to do on the farm, and it was a long way into town and to my high school." Red got a thoughtful look on his face. "I remember wanting to go out for track…I was a pretty good runner. But, the track shoes cost about ten dollars and Memo said that was too much money to spend for a pair of tennis shoes that I'd probably wear out in a few weeks!" He laughed, thinking she was probably right. "But I got to travel with the band to the games, though, and really had a lot of fun doing that."

Red pulled the car into a roadside rest station. They got out of the car and went inside to the rest rooms. When they returned to the car, Red turned to Becka.

"I've told you a lot about me, how about you?"

Becka looked at Red and smiled. "Well, what else do you want to know?"

"Do you have someone special back home, or in the service somewhere?"

"Umm, yes, I write to two guys that I know, but neither are really 'special' in the way I think you mean."

When Red did not question her further, she continued. "One is a neighbor boy I've known since childhood, and the other was my boss when I worked as a secretary in Washington. He's a terrific guy, but we're not engaged, or even 'spoken' for," Becka smiled, "How about you?" she said looking at him. "Do you have anyone special?"

"Oh, not really," said Red, "there's this gal from college – she writes to me and I see her when I visit my Aunt Scootie in Illinois. We, Marilyn and I, attended college together, and Memo crocheted a scarf for her, but, as you said, we are not 'spoken' for," Red laughed.

Red pulled Becka close to him and kissed her. "So you see, my little Kentucky gal, we are both free, no strings attached anywhere!"

They continued to drive up the coast toward Laguna Beach. Red pulled into a small restaurant called the Sea Grotto and they went inside for dinner. Becka had always loved seafood, and really enjoyed the clam chowder, sea bass and seafood salad. The dinner was served with hot garlic rolls and butter.

They lingered over dinner, each having a glass of wine, and continued to talk about their childhoods and experiences they'd had in school. Becka told Red about her best friend Hilda, and the long bike rides they took together as young teenagers.

"My junior year in school, our class took a field trip to Washington, D.C. I never dreamed at that time, that I would be working there in a few years!" She also told Red about the evening shift, where she went to work at 4 p.m. and worked until 11 p.m. "I was scared to death of walking home along that dark street after getting off the streetcar. And my fears were justified. One night as I was walking alone, a man grabbed me."

"My God, Becka, what did you do?" Red looked at her with real concern.

"Well, I can laugh about it now, but it sure wasn't funny then. When I tried to scream he covered my mouth with his hand. I twisted quickly and brought my knee up between his legs, and with my free hand, I jabbed my key into his eye. He grunted and let me go and I screamed bloody murder. He gave me a hard shove, and ran away as lights began to come on in the houses around us." Becka shivered slightly at the memory.

Red whistled, and pulled Becka close. "My Lord, honey," he whispered, "You could have been killed! I'm so glad you kept your wits about you and fought back!"

Having Red's arms about her felt great. Becka snuggled closer as she said quietly, "I called the police, but they only took my name and asked me to 'file a report' the next day. Can you believe it? That varmint got away as clean as a whistle. As far as I know he's gone on preying on women," she shuddered. "Anyway, I told my boss about the incident, and he introduced me to another girl who worked there. She was looking for a place, so I asked her to move in with me. She did, and we felt a little safer after that. We still carried our keys as 'weapons' and walked down the middle of the street instead of using the shrub-sided sidewalks. There were few cars in the neighborhood that time of night."

Becka went on to explain to Red about the neighborhood, her work, the end of the evening shift, and being transferred to a day job. They laughed together as she told him about her "encounter with the Navy" and spilling coffee all over Admiral Nimitz.

"I guess they thought I was a disaster waiting to happen!"

Red smiled. "It sounds to me as though you had a lot of fun working in Washington, D.C. Why did you transfer to the West Coast?"

Becka decided not to tell Red about Bill being in Hawaii, and her hope that he would be able to come to California on leave.

"Well, I wanted to travel and found out there was a job opening at El Toro, so I applied, and by golly, I got the job!" Becka wondered why she did not want to tell Red about Bill, and her feelings for the young Navy man who had been her boss. Oh well. She snuggled closer to Red. I'll think about that later, not now.

As they drove into Laguna Beach, Red told Becka he was sure glad she had decided to move to the West Coast. "I'm glad too," Becka answered. And they both knew why, and that they were "falling for each other" As it was late, Red said goodnight and left Becka at the door of her apartment. He had an early flight the next day.

He was also thinking about what he had heard at the squadron this past week. He had not told Becka about it, and maybe he should, he thought. Well, it would keep and he had a date with her for dinner tomorrow night.

Becka showered, washed and dried her long silky hair, creamed her face and hands and climbed into bed. She lay awake a long time, thinking. As she stared into the darkness of her room she saw a Corsair fighter plane. It was in trouble. The plane circled and circled the landing field. For some reason it was unable to make a landing. Cold sweat broke out on Becka's face. She had not had one of these "dreams" in a while. Her heart pounded and she felt a deep chill.

"Oh Lord," she prayed, "protect the pilot in that plane, bring him down safely."

In her "dream" she could not see the face of the pilot, but she felt his fear, nevertheless. She finally drifted into a troubled sleep, and awoke the next morning with slight headache, and a feeling of dread. Again she prayed silently for the unknown pilot. She knew that "somewhere" probably close by, was a pilot in trouble. If only there was something she could do to help. But she had had these "if only" feelings so many times in the past, and was unable to do anything. It was so unfair, she thought. Why do I have these "dreams" and unable to help, or change the outcome? Why?

Becka caught the shuttle bus to the Base the next morning, and had trouble concentrating on her work.

"Is something wrong?" asked her boss, Major Mooney. He had noticed the girl's nervousness, and her lack of the usual cheerfulness.

"I'm sorry Sir," answered Becka, "I guess I'm a little tired today."

"That's OK. Why don't you take an early break?" he offered with a smile. She nodded and left for the ladies' lounge.

As she walked down the long corridor to the lounge, she heard the roar of the fighter planes coming from the nearby field. Then she heard the most dreaded sound of all, the wail of sirens! Becka turned and ran back to the office. Everyone was at the windows nearest to the field, and all were looking toward the sky where a fighter plane was circling the field.

"The pilot's having trouble with the landing gear," someone said to no one in particular. Someone else remarked that the tower was urging the pilot to jump, but that he refused, not wishing the plane to crash into homes.

"He has only two choices," thought Becka, "bail out and use the parachute, or crash land!"

She found herself, along with the whole office crew, praying for this unknown pilot to "make the right choice."

"They're bringing in the fire trucks and laying down a foam runway! He's going to belly land!" someone shouted.

The office staff watched in terrified fascination as the plane came down toward the foam runway. When it got close to the ground, it seemed to drop suddenly and hit the runway hard. It bounced up and down several times and then skidded away out of view of the office windows. Those watching were unsure if the pilot had gotten out alive. They had seen no explosion, and all were hoping for the best.

Becka could not get her "dream" out of her mind as she rode home on the shuttle bus. She fervently hoped Red would come early so she might learn more about the crash. He was to pick her up at about six, so she quickly showered and dressed for dinner.

But he did not come. Becka began to have chills and forebodings. At approximately 8 p.m. she heard his step on the stair. She ran to the door and threw it open. When she saw Red standing there, she threw her arms around him and almost caused him to fall down the stairs!

"Whoa! Gal," Red laughed, "are you trying to scuttle me?"

Becka pulled him inside the apartment. "Did you hear about the crash today?" she asked quickly,

"Yes," answered Red.

"Did you know the pilot?"

"Yes," answered Red."

"Do I know him?"

"Yes," answered Red, "you know him."

"Was he hurt?" asked Becka.

"No," Red laughed. "He wasn't hurt, but the plane has some major damage to the landing gear, prop and belly."

"Oh, I'm so glad he wasn't hurt! Tell me, tell me who he is!" Becka grabbed Red's hands.

"Me," Red said simply.

"Oh, my Lord, I prayed for the pilot to have a safe landing." She sat down quickly on the sofa. "Oh, Red, I'm so glad you made it safely. I had a dream about a plane in trouble, but I woke up before the end of it, and I, well, I've been worried all day!"

Red sat down beside her and gathered her in his arms. Her cheeks were wet with tears. "Oh honey, I'm alright.

These things happen."

He kissed her wet cheeks and found her mouth. He held her for a long time, thinking how precious she was and how precious, and fragile their lives were. Inwardly he cursed the war, and wished for it to end. He wanted this beautiful little girl, he wanted to marry her and care for her, forever.

But was it fair to her, with him still in the service and with another tour of duty in the Pacific hanging over his head? He had intended to tell her that he would soon be transferred to the Night Fighter Squadron, probably at Cherry Point, North Carolina, or perhaps, Florida. But, he thought that now wouldn't be the right moment to tell her this.

"I'm sorry, Red," Becka said, wiping her eyes and blowing her nose. "I'm behaving like a child but, well, I just can't help it. I'm trying, but it is hard. Tell me about the crash. How did you land without wheels, and did the plane catch fire?"

"To answer the last first, no it didn't catch fire, thank God, and I belly-landed. I slid to a stop on the runway. It tore up the fuselage section and the prop, but I was unhurt. A fire truck came up beside the plane as soon as it stopped, and so help me if a great big burly fireman didn't reach in the cockpit and pull me out as if I was as light as a rag doll! He just lifted me right out of that cockpit as easily as slipping a banana out of its peel…and I weight about 190 pounds, so I'm no feather!" Red laughed at the memory, and felt eternally grateful to that very strong, young man. "You see, Becka," Red continued, "The safety crew had laid down about fifty feet of foam on the runway before I set the plane down. The foam retarded the chance of fire."

Red went over the events of the day in his mind. He had talked to the control tower about bailing out, but was reluctant to do so, because he didn't want the plane to crash into homes or buildings on the ground, and he didn't want to lose the plane if he could salvage it. He had told the tower that he believed he could set it down safely on the runway in a belly landing. They had told him to keep circling until they had laid down the foam, and got the emergency crews ready. It had been a tense few minutes, but it seemed that they had things in readiness very quickly. He had tried all the methods he knew to get the wheels down, but it was no use.

Red shook his head as he recalled an earlier incident. During his first tour in combat he'd had similar trouble, only that time it was one wheel up and locked, and the other down and locked.

There'd been a dog fight and his oil pressure was dropping. He pointed his nose toward home, but knew he wasn't going to make it, and started looking around for a soft patch of water. As an afterthought he lowered his gear, thinking it might give him a little more cushion. But the tower'd said no, advising him to belly in "gear up," and when he tried, one of them stuck. So there he was, one up, and one down. And that engine wasn't sounding any better either.

Where he'd just been, bailing out or crash landing wasn't an option. He'd have gone down right in the center of the island…behind enemy lines. It wasn't much better over the ocean, but he wouldn't have the Japanese to contend with. Besides, water was water, and trees were…well, hard.

Over the radio he confirmed his intention to set the plane down and requested a rescue vessel, then spent the next couple of minutes wondering if he could circle until the PT boat arrived.

Red was an excellent swimmer and wasn't afraid that he wouldn't be able to get out of the plane. Problem was, while he'd gotten a little farther from the island, he was still too close (as red tracers occasionally reminded him). Just as any predator goes after a wounded animal, the Japanese were now shooting at him from a shore battery. Red knew that once he went in the water, bingo, they'd have his range.

"Hey Dunc. Need some help?" came a friendly voice over the radio.

"Yeah, Dunc," another voice chimmed in, "get your tail feathers a mite singed?"

Tex George and Eugene "Genie" Dillard had heard Red's first call and "came a runnin'," as Genie later said.

The PT boat was close aboard so they pealed off and began strafing the shoreline, effectively stopping the ground fire. Coming back, they were just in time to see Red put his plane in the water.

"Don't get seasick" and "Don't forget you raincoat" crackled over the radio as Red glided his plane to a stall just above the waves. He killed the engine and the plane flopped in the water. Sliding the canopy back, Red jumped out, walked out to the end of the wing and dove in. After a quick couple of strokes he looked back— just in time to see the tail going under.

Floats like a rock, he thought.

A combat photographer on the PT boat had filmed the entire incident.

"That landing was perfect, Lieutenant," he'd said with excitement, "textbook! This will probably be used later as a training film."

Red had been plucked out of the choppy currents in record time. He was wet and had a bump on his head from the instrument panel, but was otherwise unhurt.

"I've been damn lucky, honey." He said to Becka after

relating the experience.

"I guess so,"

Becka shuddered, thinking about what Red was telling her. My God, she prayed silently, when will this awful war end? And he makes light of things, but I know it can't be that easy.

"So, have you been keeping Genie a secret? Am I going to get to meet him too?" Becka asked, trying to shift to another subject.

The look in Red's eyes changed, and at the same time a shadow seemed to come over his face.

"Genie was killed," he said, standing up. He went to the window and looked out at the ocean for a few moments before continuing. "His plane was in a landing pattern…500 feet…and the wing came off."

Standing, Becka went to his side and took his hand.

"It's alright," he said. "I'm okay now," He smiled slightly and put his arm around her. "That was about six months ago. Tex and Genie and I were pretty close, that's all," He looked down into her eyes. "It was pretty hard on Tex, too," he finished.

Red was holding her close now. As he related these things to Becka he knew that it was probably good for him to talk about it…but it wasn't easy. And it's probably hard for her to hear these things, he thought. I know she's worried about her brothers.

"Say, Sweetheart," Red said softly. "Let's not talk about war anymore tonight. Let's have some coffee and a piece of that chocolate cake you baked. I'm hungry as a bear!"

Becka smiled at him and went into the tiny kitchen where she prepared some sandwiches and coffee and sliced some of the chocolate cake. They sat together at her small table and ate the late supper, talked about mundane things, and didn't mention the war again. Nevertheless, it was ever-present, always on both their minds.

Becka tried to think of something funny and far removed from war and its horrors. She remembered her father's 50th birthday, and the fun their family had that evening.

"When I was a little girl," Becka said to Red, grinning at him, "I remember my Dad's 50th birthday. It was a silly custom in our family to put the 'birthday' child under the bed. We all— including Mom—decided to grab Dad when he got home from work, and put HIM under the bed!

"We hid outside on the front porch. When Dad got home he picked up the paper and walked out on the porch, intending to sit on the swing and read the paper. As he walked toward the porch swing, the three boys, Sis, Mom and I all grabbed him. There was a giant tussle, and the upshot of it was that he put all of US under the bed, including Mom!" Becka laughed remembering, and Red joined in her laughter.

"Your family sounds so great," said Red, "I never had the experience of a big family, and really never had a father in the sense that you have a Dad."

Becka and Red cleaned up the dishes and tidied the kitchen. They sat on the sofa, holding each other and talking until almost midnight. Red had felt himself gradually relaxing and his nerves quieting after his experience of that day. Lord, he thought, this little girl is so good for me. I really have to tell her about the upcoming transfer – but not tonight.

After Red left, Becka showered and climbed onto the studio couch bed. Her mind was a whirl. She had feelings about this man that she had never felt for anyone else. She pictured Bill Haulk in her mind. Where was he? She hadn't heard from him in over a month. She prayed he was safe, wherever he was. She thought of her brothers, Harry and Henry, and found that her cheeks were wet with tears. She finally drifted off to sleep, and her dreams were, happily, about her childhood, and home in Kentucky.

In her dreams she saw her mother, Elizabeth, and her Dad, Benjamin, and her brothers and sister Maggie. They were all seated around the great oval table in the kitchen. They were laughing and eating Mom's wonderful apple pie and drinking hot cocoa.

The next morning Becka awoke with the memory of the dream still with her. Then she felt the reality of the war creeping into her mind again. She tried to put it in a small compartment in the back of her thoughts, and almost succeeded. It would be about 9 a.m. at home in Kentucky, she could call her mom and dad and talk to them.

She had plenty of time before she had to catch the bus for El Toro. She picked up the telephone and dialed the old familiar number. Within seconds she heard her mom's sweet voice on the other end of the line.

"Hi, Mom," Becka said in a cheerful voice. "How are you and Daddy?"

"Hello, honey," her mother said. "I didn't get a letter from you this week, so I was expecting a call!"

"I've got a lot to tell you, Mom." Becka began. "Many things are going on out here. I wrote to you about Red. Well, Red and I are seeing each other, exclusively now. I guess you could say we are 'going steady.'"

"Oh, honey, are you sure about this?" Elizabeth asked quietly. Elizabeth knew that Becka had always shied away from making any permanent commitments. She had never wanted to go steady with any boy, preferring to be free to date as she pleased.

"Yes, Mom," Becka said. "I really do care a lot for Red.

He says he loves me, but he hasn't made any commitments, yet."

"Do you love him?" Elizabeth asked.

"I think so, I've never felt this way about anyone else," Becka said, a little hesitantly. Then she abruptly changed the subject. "Have you heard from the twins?"

Her mother told her she had not heard from either of the boys for a long time, almost a month. She and Ben were getting a little worried, but knew that mail was slow when coming from the war zones. She said that the last letter from Henry had been from the front lines in France, but she had read some of his war correspondence that had been sent to the New York Times, and reprinted in the local papers.

Through his correspondence to the News she was able to keep up with his activities and whereabouts better than with Harry, who was in the Pacific theatre and moving about on the war ships. She went on to tell Becka that Harry's ship had been in a mighty battle with the Japanese fleet. Ships were sunk and many men were wounded and killed. Harry had managed to get word to them that he had survived, and spent many hours caring for wounded sailors on board his ship. His ship had received some damage, but was still under command and serviceable.

The two talked on for another few minutes. Becka bragged about the weather in Laguna Beach, and Elizabeth moaned about the nasty weather in Kentucky. Becka told her Mom that she and her Dad should come to Laguna Beach for a visit and leave the snow and icy rain behind.

"That sure sounds wonderful, honey. I wish we could," Elizabeth said wistfully.

Both Becka and her mother knew that there would be little traveling for her parents as long as her Dad was still working at the Mill. ARMCO was at full capacity production during these war years and Benjamin was a valuable employee. He was 58 years old, and expected to work until he reached 65.

"Ben will have 2 weeks vacation this year, and perhaps we can do some traveling then," Liz remarked.

"That would be great if you could come to California, but it's a long way for only 2 weeks," Becka answered.

The mother and daughter spoke a little longer and then Becka had to cut their conversation short, in order to catch the shuttle bus to the Marine Core Air Base. As soon as she hung up, she grabbed her purse and ran to the corner where the bus picked her up each morning during the week. She barely made it. The bus was pulling to her corner just as she came puffing up to the bus stop.

The bus driver grinned at Becka as she climbed aboard. "Overslept this morning?" he asked as she settled in her seat. Becka smiled at him. "Not really, I was talking to my Mom in Kentucky, and let the time slip away."

"So that's where you get that southern drawl." He laughed again. Becka laughed, too. "Now Ralph, don't go giving me a bad time about my Kentucky drawl, some folks think it's pretty cute." And Becka made a face at him that he could see in the rear view mirror.

Ralph laughed heartily. He had liked Becka from the first time she rode the bus, and the two had exchanged banter and good-natured teasing over the past few months. Ralph looked forward to seeing her each morning, and worried if she didn't show up on time, or missed a day. Becka knew the old man worried (he was only 56, but this was 'old' to Becka), so she usually told him when she had a day off, or was otherwise detained.

That morning she sat quietly, thinking. Why didn't she tell her mother more about Red? Maybe it was because she didn't have enough time. No, that wasn't it, she thought. No, she just wasn't ready to talk about her relationship with Red. Did she really have a relationship? They had not made any commitments. They had not been intimate. They had done some heavy "necking" but had not gone too far. What was it? Was Red keeping something from her? Tex had said something about being transferred. Was Red being transferred? If so, why hadn't he told her? Should she ask him about it? Should she wait? She just didn't know!

As these thoughts whirled through her mind, she realized that she hadn't told her mother more about Red, because she really didn't understand some very important things about him! She wanted to make excuses for him. Excuses such as "It has to do with war secrets," or, "His commanding officer had forbidden them to talk," and so on.

Well, she thought, I'll just have to wait until he's ready to talk to me. I'll be darned if I bring it up. The "ball is in his court" as the saying goes.

As the bus pulled up to the offices on the base, Becka caught sight of Tex. He was standing outside the office door, the door she usually entered to report for work. When she climbed down from the bus, Tex walked over and said hello.

"Got a minute," he asked, taking her hand?

Becka nodded and the two walked over to a shady area beneath a nearby tree. There were benches there and the area was often used as a nice little place to eat lunch.

"Hey, Tex" Becka said, as they sat down on the bench in the shade. "What's up? You seem to have something on your mind." She continued.

Becka was wearing a pale blue blouse and skirt. Her hair was pulled back and tied with a bow. Small strands of curls escaped and framed her face. She had little makeup on and Tex caught the light fragrance of her cologne. My God, he thought, but she is one pretty little gal! If Red doesn't "declare himself soon" I'm moving in! He took Becka's hands and gave them a light squeeze.

"God, honey, but you look good enough to eat this morning! Will you marry me?" He was only half kidding.

Becka laughed. "Oh, Tex, you are always full of it, aren't you!"

They both laughed and talked for a few more minutes, and then Becka asked him again what he wanted to talk to her about. She had a feeling she already knew.

"Well, you see Becka," Tex said quietly, "There's wind in the air that a bunch of us will be transferred soon. I just wanted you to know."

He watched her closely. She sat quietly for a moment, then looked up at him.

"Will Red be transferred also?" she asked.

"Oh, I can't say about him, I'm not supposed to know, but it ain't no secret; all the guys seem to know about it. I expect we'll be having a briefing soon."

"Do you have any idea where they're sending you?" Becka asked.

"Not really," Tex answered. "But I'll tell you when I do know, if it's permitted."

As they talked, Tex was watching Becka closely. She's in love with Red. I wonder if the lucky guy knows it. Maybe I should talk to him, or, maybe not.

Becka looked at her watch "Well, Tex, I have to get to work. Thanks for talking to me. I really appreciate it. I've had a feeling that something was in the air, I just wasn't sure what!"

She squeezed his hand and got up to leave. As she stood,

Tex leaned over and kissed her on her soft mouth. She looked up at him in surprise, and Tex blushed bright red.

"I'm sorry, Becka," he stammered, "I just couldn't help it."

Becka laughed. "It's O.K. Tex," she said, then stood on her tiptoes and kissed his cheek.

As they parted and went their separate ways to work, Becka's mind was a whirl with mixed feelings. Why hadn't Red told her, she wondered. Tex was so open about everything, and Red seemed so closed up, somehow.

Over two thousand miles to the East, Ben and Elizabeth, were sitting down to a late lunch/early dinner. It was a chilly spring day and the overhanging clouds had long since obscured the pale sun. The kitchen was warm, however, and the fragrance of fried chicken and potatoes, Ben's favorite supper, filled the room. Liz had made green beans with onions and bacon, and hot biscuits, too.

Ben was working the day shift and had arrived home about 4 p.m. He had showered at the mill, and was wearing a clean blue shirt and trousers. He read the daily news as Elizabeth prepared the early supper. He had brought in his big metal lunch pail and put it on the sideboard. Liz had opened it and removed the napkins and the remains of a sandwich she had made him for lunch. It was their daily routine, and both were comfortable with their lives. The big dog lay against the wall out of the way, and when Liz opened the lunch pail, he looked up and whined.

"Oh," laughed Liz "You'd like the rest of this sandwich, then?" And she tossed it to the dog, who caught and ate it in one gulp.

The old dog was beginning to show his age; he was getting grey around the mouth, and he moved a little slower these days. As Liz looked at the loved animal, she remembered how near death he had been from the terrible wound on his head.

Liz, Winter 1944

Becka and Sherry
Summer 1945

She thought of the day it had happened, about six weeks earlier. It had been a warm day and she was sitting on the front porch swing. She hadn't seen Brutus for a while, but thought nothing of it. The Jewel Tea salesman pulled up in front of the house. He got out of the car and walked to the porch, removing his hat and giving Liz a smile and a bow.

"Hello, there Miz Young." He said, "May I come up and sit with you for a few minutes?" His name was Thompson, and was always called "Tommy." He was about fifty years old, small framed and wiry, with dark hair graying at the temples.

Liz smiled and pushed a rocking chair over for him. She had been expecting him, as she bought tea and coffee from him once a month. As Tommy settled into the rocking chair, he looked around for the dog. One of the few outsiders that Brutus tolerated, the dog and man seemed to like each other a great deal.

"Where is Brutus?" He asked.

"You know, I haven't seen him since early this morning when the two of us fed the chickens" Liz said.

"Mmm, that's strange. He always knows when I come and comes to meet me. Maybe we'd better look for him." Tommy got out of the rocker and started around the porch, whistling for the dog as Liz walked with him, a growing apprehension in her breast.

They found Brutus lying on his side, a pool of congealed blood near his head. He was not moving.

"Oh, my heavens!" cried Liz as she ran to the dog. But Tommy was there ahead of her and stooped down and gently examined the great shaggy head.

"He's still breathing," he said to Liz. "Bring some blankets and help me get him into my car. I'll bring the car around the driveway to the back and we can put him in the back seat."

Liz ran into the house, grabbed some old army blankets and a clean towel for Brutus's head. She took her purse off the hook and ran to help Tommy lift the dog into the car. They drove into Ashland to the nearest vet's office.

Brutus had a deep cut across the top of his head and had lost a great deal of blood, but his vital signs were stable.

"Someone tried to kill your dog," the Vet said, shaking his head. "They almost succeeded. But this dog is a tough old fellow; he's going to be fine. I've put 18 stitches in his head, and given him a shot to keep him still for a while. Just give him water for today, no food, and keep him quiet." The vet then gave Liz a packet of pills for Brutus to be given each day.

As Liz remembered that day, she looked fondly at the great dog as he lay looking at her, expecting another morsel of "human food" to be thrown over to him. His shaggy tail thumped the floor and his tongue lolled out of his mouth in a great doggy smile. Liz soaked a warm biscuit in bacon gravy and put it in the dog's bowl. She gingerly patted the great head. The hair was growing back now, almost obscuring the deep red scar. She thought how thankful she was that Tommy had come just when he had, and had been there to take the dog to the vet.

As she and Ben sat down to supper, they talked briefly about the incident. Both suspected a certain neighbor of injuring the dog, but had no proof, so they could not say anything. This particular neighbor had a habit of "helping himself" to Ben's tools in the tool shed, a practice Brutus did not like. The dog would growl and bark, trapping the neighbor inside the shed, thereby forcing him to call Ben or Liz for permission to leave with the borrowed tool.

And, interestingly enough, the day they found Brutus,

they also found a bloody scythe lying on the grass near the dog. It was obvious to both, this had been the weapon used to try to kill the dog. After the incident, Ben put a padlock on the tool shed; the neighbor never again called to borrow a tool, and never again came into the yard when the dog was outside. Now, with all the children grown and away from home, Ben felt good about Brutus being there with Liz.

It was a good neighborhood. Most of the folks living around them were honest, hard working people, ready to lend a helping hand when needed. And Ben was no different. Considered the "fix-it man" in the neighborhood, if something was broken Ben "Hoss" Young could fix it, happily repairing anything from a wristwatch to a vacuum cleaner. And, most of the time he was successful. Having the proper tools for most any job in his tool shed, he kept them oiled and organized as neatly as would a surgeon with the tools of his trade.

Well educated with certificates in Engineering, mining engineering, and electrical engineering, Ben had a keen mind and was an excellent mathematician. He would delight his children by adding large sums in his head, and saying the alphabet backward. He had a droll sense of humor, and Liz said he couldn't say a word if his hands were tied behind him!

This afternoon, as Ben finished off the last piece of fried chicken, he winked at Liz. "I think I married the best cook in the State of Kentucky!"

Liz leaned over and kissed his cheek. She said she would finish the dishes as Ben went out to see about the chickens. They did not keep a cow or pigs, but Liz enjoyed having chickens, and each year ordered a new batch of chicks from Sears and Roebuck's. As she washed the dishes in hot soapy water, she remembered little Becka making pets of the chickens, and being spanked for disobeying her and making a pet of "big Red," the rooster.

Liz's mind filled with thoughts of Becka, now a grown young woman, living so far away out in California. What a capable young woman she had turned out to be. But Liz worried about Becka's soft heart and trusting nature. Becka had told her a little about Red, her new "boyfriend," and Liz suspected that her daughter was more than just "fond" of him. "Oh Lord," she prayed silently, "take care of her; don't let her get her heart broken."

She worried, as did all mothers, that this "Red" would hurt her daughter, or break her heart, but the worry went deeper. Red, Liz knew, was a Marine Fighter pilot and that his work was dangerous and risky. She knew also that as this awful war was lagging on and on. This young man, as well as many of her neighbors' sons, and indeed her own sons, Harry and Henry, were in constant, mortal danger.

After the dishes were done, Liz went into their bedroom and shut the door. She knelt down beside the bed and prayed for all the boys in the services, as well as her own sons Harry and Henry. And Becka...and Red. Of course, she had never met Red, but Becka had told her about him, and Liz admired what he did. And, she was somewhat in awe of the skill needed to fly a Corsair, let alone "dogfight" with Japanese Zeros.

"I hope Becka calls again soon." Liz remarked, "I'm anxious to hear more about her new boyfriend. I have the feeling that it is more than she is saying,"

She and Ben were sitting on the couch in the living room. They had the radio turned on and were listening to the news. They always listened to Lowell Thomas. His news reports were generally accurate and at the end of each news report he usually told a funny story or an uplifting account of some happening at the war front.

As they were listening and Thomas finished the war news, he said, "And Lt. Henry Robert Ernest Young of Ashland, Kentucky found out recently that a bullet in the hand is better than one through the hand. As Young was standing near his bunker somewhere in France, a sniper's bullet hit his rifle barrel and deflected flat into the palm of his hand. It was hot, though spent, and he quickly dropped it. His buddies call him "superman" for catching a bullet in his hand!"

Ben and Liz were spellbound at this unexpected "news" about Henry. He had not written them in sometime, and they were both surprised and concerned to hear this news, even if it was on the amusing side of the report.

Thousands of miles away in a small grove of trees somewhere in France, Henry and his company had stopped for a few days. They were temporarily out of immediate danger and had called a halt for a day or two of rest. Apparently, however, they were not completely safe from snipers as Henry found out when the sniper had shot at him and hit his rifle barrel. The bullet had hit his hand and Henry felt the heat, but no pain. He picked up the bullet and showed it to his buddies. There had been much teasing about "superman," and Henry had bored a hole through the bullet and hung it around his neck, where it remained throughout the rest of his combat duty.

A mobile kitchen unit had moved up to the small-forested area where the men were resting and the cook prepared hot meals for the men—a real treat considering the K-Rations they usually ate. There was a fast running creek near the area and the cook went down to get water to make coffee and soup. The men found a dead cow near the spot where the cook had obtained the water. Some of the men complained to the cook about this, however, the cook just shrugged.

"That there dead cow was downstream from where I got the water," he said, "so you men just quit your bellyaching!"

Fortunately, none of the men got ill from eating the food…"stray" chickens in this case, liberated by the cook himself, and they'd made a delicious chicken vegetable soup.

One man had rescued a starving dog he found wandering and hungry in the woods. He was skin and bones, and almost dead from hunger. The men fed him and named him "Bullet." The dog was a German Sheppard and stayed with the men through the balance of their stay at the war front. Bullet proved a valuable asset to the men, warning them of danger. The commanding officer of the unit commissioned the dog, making him a "Sergeant Guard Dog."

Henry wrote a story about the dog in some of his war correspondence as Bullet had become quite well known and respected by all the men. He received much attention and affection, and returned the men's kindness by becoming a real guard dog. During the weeks and months the dog was with the men he was wounded twice, and was given a purple heart and cited for bravery.

In Ashland, Ben and Liz re-read a letter they had recently received from Harry. He had written them about some of his experiences on the ship, his duties as a medical officer, and some of the more humorous things that had happened to him. However, his days were busy with wounded men, lack of sleep and the trauma of being unable to save some of the wounded sailors. Both Harry and Henry had become seasoned and capable adults, doing their respective jobs with efficiency and courage. Their parents were very proud of the twins, and prayed for them each day.

As Harry sat near a wounded sailor late one night aboard the ship, he thought of the time he and Henry had operated on the chicken. A smile crossed his tired face as the memory flooded back. The chicken in question had swallowed a ball of twine and part of it was now hanging out it's beak. The poor thing couldn't eat and was starving to death.

Harry decided to operate.

So, while their parents were out, they took brandy from their Pa's cabinet, and using an eyedropper, gave the chicken enough brandy to get her "stinking drunk." Once "anesthetized," they tied the unresisting chicken to the ironing board and proceeded to operate on her gullet.

While Henry held the bird down, Harry carefully cut open the craw. Upon revealing the tightly wound, offending ball of string, the boys removed it, sewed up the craw with a needle and black thread, and gently placed the hen back on her nest. By the next morning, to the delight of both boys, the hen was out in the chicken yard pecking up the corn with the other chickens! The surgery had been a great success.

And this had not been the only time the boys had decided to play doctor. A wry smile touched the corners of Harry's mouth as he recalled another of their "secret" incidents. The boys had been playing with their BB guns at the "Spider Club," a "hideout" located down in a hollow near their home. And, as occasionally happens with boys of that age, Harry had been accidentally shot by a BB gun. Barely missing his right eye, the BB had struck his nose, slid under the skin, and traveled down the side of his nose to his cheek.

"This BB'll have to be removed," Harry pronounced, rubbing his forefinger gingerly along his nose. "If Ma or Pa finds out about this…they will take our guns away,:. ”

"…. they'll take the guns away for sure," Henry finished.

This was something they both considered a fate worse than death…certainly worth the minor amount of pain required to remove a small, copper ball.

In grim preparation, Henry "sanitized" his Boy Scout knife with a large kitchen match. Then, solomnly giving Harry a stick to put between his teeth (you had to put a stick between your teeth…it was in all the movies), Henry carefully sliced open his brother's cheek and removed the BB. Unfortunately it was such a small, shallow incision that Henry did not need to "sew it up" (much as he wanted to). He was able to satisfied himself, however, with the squirms and groans accompanying the antisceptic he so generously applied to the wound.

That night at the dinner table, their Mother asked what in the world had happened to Harry's face. Harry just shrugged and said he had run into some berry bushes and cut himself. Liz took him to the sink, washed his face with soap and water, and once again iodine was applied to the cut. And, once again, this hurt worse than the "surgery!"

At the recollection of these escapades of their youth, Harry had an overwhelming feeling of loneliness for his twin brother. The two boys had been so close as youngsters. Now, they were so far apart. Harry silently prayed that Henry was O.K wherever he was.

The young, seriously wounded sailor stirred and moaned bringing Harry quickly back to the present. Going to his side, Harry quickly administered pain medication and stayed with the young man until he again fell asleep.

And there he would remain through all of the long hours until the first streaks of dawn filtered through the misty clouds surrounding the great battleship. Then, as another corpsman would relieve him, Harry would wearily make his way to the galley, there to drink coffee and eat an orange or two before going to his bunk for some badly needed sleep.

Far across the Pacific in Laguna Beach, Becka was reading a letter from her big sister, Maggie. As luck would have it, Johnny was being transferred to The Pentagon in Washington, D.C.

Only completed the previous year (mid January, 1943), the building was enormous—in fact the world's highest capacity office building. In later years the Pentagon would become synonymous with The Department of Defense, but for now, Johnny would work it's war offices as a Budget Officer.

Maggie was happy about the move, and had been accepted as a teacher in a high school in nearby Falls Church, Virginia. She also wrote that Johnny intended to continue his education by attending the George Washington University in D.C. there to get his degree in accounting.

During the Great Depression Maggie had worked herself nearly to death in her effort to finish college. Only a child at the time, Becka nevertheless remembered those years, and her sister's long struggle of studying and teaching at the same time, and almost "going under" from the stress and strain. Sitting at her little writing desk, Becka composed a letter to Maggie, congratulating her on the move, and writing that she knew she and Johnny would "love" Washington, D.C.

And the prediction had been right. Maggie did love the Nation's Capital and all it had to offer. Excitement, new experiences, and her new proximity to all of the wonderful art galleries, museums, monuments; she would visit them all. As a teacher of art, math, and music at the local high school, Maggie would become very popular indeed, directing the orchestra, planning drama events, and working on the yearbooks. She would continue teaching in Falls Church for the next 30 years.

Having also heard the news, in Kentucky, Ben and Elizabeth were planning a trip to Washington to help Maggie with moving and getting settled in her new home in Falls Church. A large brick and stone house, it had ample space for all of their books, art supplies, John's tools, as well as room for overnight guests. Upon her arrival, Elizabeth loved the house and delighted in helping Maggie settle in. Later she had fun exploring the great city of Washington, D.C. with her daughter while Ben and Johnny visited the place where Johnny would work.

On Sunday they all attended the church services. The young couple was welcomed to the church and immediately felt a part of the congregation. During the following years Maggie became the piano accompanist for the choir and Johnny taught Sunday school classes.

Ben and Elizabeth visited Maggie as often as possible during the war years. Because of the shortage of gasoline and gasoline rationing, they usually took the Greyhound bus to Falls Church. It was a 10 to 12 hour trip. Both Ben and Liz enjoyed the bus trip for it gave them time to talk and look out the bus window at the lovely West Virginia and Virginia mountains and rivers.

Because Ben was a long time employee of ARMCO, he was able to get extra time off during the year. He took part of Friday off on the weekends they visited Maggie. This gave them almost three days for a weekend in Falls Church.

They often went to visit Will, in nearby Boston, as well. Liz delighted in the grandchildren and she and Ben enjoyed the delicious old-fashioned cooking Will's wife loved to serve. Will's wife, a vibrant young woman with dark hair and a beautiful smile, cooked the way her husband liked to eat: fried chicken, lots of mashed potatoes and gravy, and home made bread.

After a weekend visit to Maggie's home, Liz had written Becka that Maggie was considering adopting a baby. Evidently a young woman had recently given birth to a little boy, and her husband, having been shipped overseas was now missing in action. The young woman, needing to work, could not adequately care for the child, and as an aquaintance of theirs, John and Maggie had agreed to care for the baby. Shortly thereafter, they agreed to adopt him.

Liz had held the little boy and found him a delight, with big blue eyes and handsome features. Now, as Becka read the letter from her mother, she could just picture Maggie holding the tiny youngster, cuddling him…loving him. Becka knew that Maggie wanted children, but had never gotten pregnant and Becka hoped this would work out for her big sister and for Johnny.

March slid into April and brought springtime to Laguna Beach. Red, Becka and often Tex (and his "latest") continued to see each other. The four went bowling, to movies, picnics and spent long lazy days on the beach. Becka teased Red because he rarely put on swim trunks but wore a full set of khakis when he sat on the beach or swam. When he went into the surf he slipped off his long pants, wearing his swim trunks underneath, but keeping on the long sleeved shirt.

Having the true complexion of a redhead, Red would get fierce burns if he did not "cover up," and was openly envious of Tex's ability to get a deep tan. Tex had skin that tanned to a rich golden brown, and he was very handsome with his deep tan, his dark curly hair and twinkling brown eyes.

Each time that Becka and Tex were together where they could talk without Red hearing them, Tex would ask

Becka if Red had told her about the rumored move of their squadron. Becka shook her head sadly. She did not understand why Red had not spoken to her about this, and it was affecting their relationship. During the third week of April, Tex came into Red's room at the Officer's Quarters. Red was getting dressed for a date with Becka.

"Hey, Dunc," Tex began with a wide grin "When are you gonna ask that beautiful little gal to marry you?" He went on before Red could answer, "If you don't ask her soon, I'm gonna beat you to it!"

Red paused as he tied his shoelaces. He looked at Tex without smiling.

"Are you in love with Becka, " Red asked, very softly.

"Hells Bells, Dunc!" Tex answered. "Who isn't?"

The two had been close friends from the time they first met as squadron buddies, and Tex immediately realized that Red was serious…very serious. And he loved the guy. Hell, they were brothers…might as well have been, anyway, and Tex didn't want to cause any strained relationships between them.

And the same thoughts were going through Red's mind. He'd always wanted a "real" brother. While he had a young, half-brother, Red hardly knew him.

Tex leaned over and slapped Red on the back, "You know, don't you, that I realize that you're in love with her? "I just can't understand why you are draggin' your feet!"

Red looked at Tex and the smile returned to his face.

"Well, Tex" he drawled, "I just can't find the right time, with this squadron move coming up, I'm afraid, you know, I'm afraid she'll say no." And Red had an anguished expression on his face.

"Well," drawled Tex, "Don't wait too long. I hear we're going to make a move soon…and to the East Coast."

Red had heard the same rumor and knew that he

couldn't keep the news from Becka much longer. He had a feeling that she already knew something was up.

That evening when he arrived at Becka's apartment, she was not quite ready. She told him to come in, have some coffee, and apologized for making him wait. She disappeared into the small dressing room to complete her make-up. As she returned to the room, Red was standing at the dressing room door. He pulled her into his arms and began to kiss her. Becka gently pushed him back to the lounge and they both sat down.

Red took both her hands in his. "Becka," he said very quietly, "I'm being transferred to the East Coast. I don't want to leave you. Will I have to tie you up to take you with me?"

Becka pulled him close and kissed him "You won't have to tie me up, darling, I'll go with you."

"Do you mean it? You'll marry me?" Red asked, delighted.

He reached into his pocket and brought a small pink box. He handed it to Becka, holding it ever so gently, as though it was a precious gem. And indeed it was. As she opened the small beautifully decorated box, she found a lovely diamond engagement ring.

"Oh, Red," she exclaimed in excitement. Tears were streaming down her face. "It is so very lovely. Will you put it on my finger?"

As Red slipped the ring on her finger, his own eyes were misty. "Becka" he said softly, "I've wanted to tell you about the impending move, and to ask you to marry me, but somehow, well, I just wasn't sure you'd be happy about it."

Becka was quiet for a long moment, and then she put her arms around Red and kissed him. "I've known for a long time, several weeks, in fact, that the squadron was going to move. I just couldn't understand why you never told me."

"How did you know? Red asked. "Did Tex tell you?"

"Yes, he did, but I had heard about it before Tex told me. Many people here on the base knew, and talked about it. It didn't seem to be a secret."

"Why didn't you say something?" Red asked, looking perplexed.

"Well, I guess I felt a little like you said you were feeling. You know, not sure about talking to you on the subject."

They both laughed, and Red pulled Becka to him and kissed her, long and hard. "Come on, gal" he said with a wide smile, "Let's go have dinner and celebrate!"

Her children rise up and call her blessed

Proverbs: 31

DO YOU REMEMBER, SISTER, BROTHERS

How we used to run and play
In the shady apple orchard
On those warm sun shiny days?
Those first warm days of summer
When we ran without a care
Barefoot and lighthearted
Calling out to have our share
Of fresh green apples tart and juicy,
And the games of hound and hare?
Mother calling us to supper,
Daddy coming home from work
The round table in the kitchen
Hot apple cobbler – What luck!
The days have passed so quickly
The years are swiftly gone
And time has changed so much
Since now we all are grown
It's good to reminisce
In the September of our years,
Those days of glorious springtime
The joys and the tears.
Greetings to you, Sister, Brothers,
While in miles we're far apart
We are still so close in memory
We are still so close in heart.

CHAPTER TEN

The Family 1944 – 1962

BECKA GOT up the next morning before dawn. She couldn't wait to tell her parents! It had been too late the night before, as her parents would have been in bed, asleep, by the time she and Red returned from dinner.

"Hello Mom," she began, as her mother's voice came over the phone. "I've got something to tell you. I hope you'll be happy for me."

"Well, good morning, darling. It's so good to hear your voice," said Liz. "Now what's this good news?" She motioned for Ben to pick up the other telephone.

"Oh Mom!...and Dad!...are you there too, Daddy? Well, I have a beautiful diamond ring on the third finger of my left hand. Red asked me to marry him, and I said yes! And guess what, he's being transferred to the East Coast. We plan to be married before he leaves, and I'm going with him!"

Becka was so excited that her words were tumbling over

themselves. Liz and Ben could hardly keep up with her.

"Hold on Sweetie," Ben broke in, laughing, "Slow down."

The three talked for several more minutes until Becka had to stop and get ready for work. She told them she was so happy that she would probably not need to ride the bus; she felt she could "just fly all the way!!"

Becka caught the shuttle bus and thirty minutes later she was at the base. She looked for Tex who had often been waiting for her when she reached the bus stop, but today he was not there. She felt disappointed, want so much to tell him the news and show him her ring.

Becka, who was often insightful and intuitive about other people's feelings, did not realize the depth of Tex's feelings for her. She looked at her relationship with Tex as like a "good friend" — almost as a brother. She and Tex had talked many times, but he always seemed to be joking or teasing when the conversation turned to serious matters.

She never had the courage to ask him about the terrible scar that ran from his eyebrow down to his chin. Upon asking Red, however, she learned that Tex had been seriously injured during their first tour in combat. His plane had been shot up and he'd gone down in the jungle, and while the Marines on the ground had rescued him, he'd been unconscious and in a coma for several weeks.

"Oh, the doctors stitched him up," Red explained, "and, he had gradually recovered, but he had blurred vision in his left eye and they told him he could never fly in combat again."

Watching Red's face as he related the story, Becka began to understand

"It was a devastating blow to Tex," Red continued. "more

than anything else, he wanted to stay with the squadron…"

"Just as you're doing," Becka interjected.

"I suppose so," Red agreed, nodding. "He wanted to return with the squadron to the South Pacific…and into combat."

Red understood Tex's bitter feelings, and worried about his attitude. He'd tried to cheer his friend up by telling him his blurred vision might clear up.

"You'll be back in there," Red would say, "giving the enemy hell, again."

But Tex remained discouraged and unhappy. Of course he never deminstrated any of these feelings when he was with Becka. He was always his seemingly light-hearted self.

Because Red didn't know the exact date of the move, Becka did not tell her boss about her engagement, nor that she would be leaving with Red. However, she had worn the ring and several of her co-workers noticed it.

"Hey, Beck" said one of the co-workers as the two girls were working together in the file room, "What's that on your finger? It's beautiful!"

Becka smiled and said, quietly, although she wanted to shout it, "I'm engaged. To Red."

"Oh, Beck, I'm so happy for you!" and the two girls laughed and hugged.

Of course the news spread throughout the office, and presently Becka's boss, called her into his office. Becka had taken her pad and pencil into the office, but Major Moody, shook his head.

"Sit down, Becka, you won't need to take notes now, I just wanted to talk." And he smiled and motioned her to sit. "What's all this scuttlebutt I've been hearing? Am I the last one to know?"

Becka looked at her boss with real affection. She had

liked him from the first day she had reported for work and would be truly sorry to leave.

"I'm really sorry, Sir," she said, and meant it. "I intended to tell you as soon as I knew for sure, you know, for sure when I'd be leaving."

"Well, I see that sparkler on your finger. Who's the lucky guy?" and he gave her a broad smile.

Becka returned the smile and blushed slightly. "Red, I mean Captain Warren Duncan, Sir. We plan to be married soon."

"Does this mean you'll be leaving us?" Major Moody asked, knowing the answer already. He knew about the squadron's plans, of course. But, he didn't know the exact time. It might be a week or several weeks. He was not privileged to the total "scoop."

"I know the Captain," he went on, "he is a great guy, and incidentally, a fine pilot. Congratulations and my very best wishes." He stood up and reached his hand to Becka, who took it with a slight curtsy and a charming smile.

As soon as Becka found out the date of the move, she informed Major Moody. Some of the office staff planned a going away party for Becka, combined with a bridal shower. They planned the party for the lunch hour and decorated the large conference room. (Major Moody had agreed that the event could be during a time when the conference room would not be in use).

The party was a great success! The girls strung paper ribbons and balloons around the room as well as other special decorations. A large bowl of fresh flowers adorned the long table. Janet, a special friend, brought them from her own garden. And gifts! Becka received many lovely things – linens, towels, silverware, beautiful picture frames and personal items such as frilly nightgowns, perfume, and so on.

Thrilled and delighted with the party, Becka thanked everyone, saying she was truly sorry to leave them, and promised to write and keep in touch.

Becka kept her promise, for she corresponded with these special friends for many years.

Becka called her parents, telling them about the shower and that the tentative date of the planned wedding would be May 2nd. Elizabeth's sister, Lou, lived in Phoenix, Arizona. She now lived with friends as her husband had passed away some years earlier. Now Becka called her Aunt and the two spoke about the wedding plans, with Aunt Lou as a special attendant. Telling her aunt that she and Red planned to arrive as early as possible on May 2nd, Lou then called her pastor at the Episcopalian Church to perform the wedding.

Becka was thrilled and happy that someone as special as her mother's sister could be with her on this very wonderful day, and asked Red if he wanted to invite his grandmother. Red, however, said he preferred to "surprise" her with a visit as they traveled through Texas to Midland, where his grandmother lived.

The Saturday before Red and Becka left for Phoenix, they met Tex and his girlfriend, Cindy, at a local restaurant for dinner. Tex was his usual self, teasing Red and joking with Becka, and saying he wanted to go to the wedding, but couldn't make it.

"Becka," he said, with his special smile and wink, "if this big red-headed mug ever 'does you wrong' you just call me, you hear?"

Red laughed and gave Tex a friendly punch on the arm. "Don't worry, ole Buddy I'm taking extra good care of this little lady."

Red had realized sometime earlier that Tex was in love

with Becka. He knew that Tex, whose feelings were supposedly hidden, wanted them to be happy. Damn it to hell, thought Red, why do we have to be in love with the same girl? He felt he should be able to say something to Tex, but didn't know how to express himself.... or even if he should.

The four young people kept the conversation in a light tone, laughing and joking throughout the dinner. They didn't want to end the evening and decided to take a moonlight walk on the beach. They found an unused fire ring and Red and Tex soon had a cheery fire going. The sand was warm from the day's sun and the four sat around the fire, talking and enjoying each other's company until almost midnight. Becka sat close to Red who kept his arm around her. Tex and Cindy were snuggled close and none of them noticed the tall figure that walked up to their fire ring.

"What in the hell do you think you're doing?" said a rough male voice. The four looked up to see a uniformed figure standing over them. "You guys should know better!" he fairly shouted at them.

Red jumped to his feet. "Oh Hell, officer," he said quickly. "Our only excuse is, well, I guess, love. You see, this little lady and I just got engaged, and I completely forgot about the light blackout." As he was talking he was throwing sand on the fire, putting out the flames. Tex had jumped to his feet also, and was adding sand to the fire ring.

The officer began to laugh and helped the two men put out the fire. When they were sure only a little smoke was left, they all sat down on the sand in the moonlight, with the officer joining them. "Did you know that there was a report of a Japanese submarine prowling the shores near here?" the police officer asked.

"Damnation!" exclaimed Tex. "When was this?" he wanted to know.

Neither he nor Red had heard anything about this happening in the past month or more. They had heard that a sub was spotted during the first months of the war, but had no reports recently.

Becka whispered to Red that she was getting a little chilly and felt they should head for home. The four walked with the officer to Red's car with the officer reminding them that they should not turn on their headlights until their car was pointing away from the beach, "...and even then," he said, "turn on the low beams only."

Tex had left his car at Becka's apartment, and before they left, they promised to come over the next day and help Red and Becka get packed. True to his word, Tex showed up, alone, and proceeded to help load the car for the long journey to the East Coast.

"I wish I could go with you and be best man," Tex said with a rueful grin. "Just you remember little girl, if this big redhead doesn't treat you right, just you call me, you hear?" and Tex gave Becka a big hug and a kiss. He turned to Red and stuck out his hand. The two men shook hands and both men had misty eyes.

Several days earlier, Tex had informed Red that the commanding officer of the squadron had called him in and told him that he would not be going east with the squadron. His explanation to Tex was that Tex needed more medical attention for his blurred vision, and if his vision cleared up, he would follow them later.

"Hells bells!" Tex had exclaimed to Red, "You know that ain't gonna happen. I'm afraid I'm gonna be grounded!"

Red thought that what Tex said was probably true, however, he put his arm around Tex's shoulder, and said, "Hey, Buddy, they can't keep a crackerjack flyer like you on the ground! You'll be up there with the rest of us, giving those

Zeros hell!"

"Thanks, Dunc," Tex said with his sardonic grin, "I hope you're right." But both men felt that their optimism was in vain.

The three had packed the 1941 Ford with all Becka's things, and still had room for some of Red's uniforms and personal items. The Marines had shipped most of his things to Cherry Point, North Carolina.

When the young couple arrived in Phoenix, Aunt Lou was very happy to see them. She approved of Red, immediately, and gave him a big hug. After hugging and kissing Becka, she informed them that she had contacted the minister at her church, and he would perform the wedding at 4 p.m. that afternoon.

The home where Lou was staying was a beautiful old mansion surrounded by lovely well-kept gardens. Becka had seen gracious homes such as this in and around Washington, D.C. Mary Farnsworth, Aunt Lou's hostess and dear friend, made the young couple feel right at home. A maid brought hot coffee and sandwiches to the den and soon Becka and Red were enjoying a welcome late lunch and excitedly talking about their future plans.

Lou showed the two young people to separate rooms where they were able to shower and get dressed for the wedding. The room where Becka dressed was large with long windows looking out over the garden. The furniture was polished cherry with pale pink satin on the chairs and bedspread and matching drapes. Becka looked around the spacious room and felt very happy and special. Her mother's sister, Lou, was much loved by Becka, and she was happy for Lou that she lived in such a beautiful place.

Aunt Lou had moved out to Phoenix during the first years of her marriage to Walter. Walter's health had been poor and the doctors had advised a dry climate, feeling the move would help him improve. And it had. The move had been a wise one for Walter, for he lived many years. Walter, Lou, and family had purchased a large orange grove and the family had lived there until Walter's death a few years earlier. Lou then sold the groves and moved in with her friend Mary. Lou's two children, Daniel and Joanna were already grown and married and living out of state. Lou, who had always prided herself on being a great organizer, had, with Mary's help, planned the wedding to the last detail.

The wedding party arrived at the beautiful old church where the minister was waiting for them. He took Red and Becka into his chambers and counseled with them for about an hour. Becka was so excited and nervous that later, she could not remember anything the minister, Dean Edwin Lane had said!

When Becka and Red returned to the chapel Aunt Lou and Mary were waiting for them. Presently the minister returned. He was wearing a long gold and silver robe with a beautiful scarf around his shoulders. Becka was wearing a pale lavender suit, and the lovely white orchid Red had bought for her, looked beautiful pinned on her shoulder. Red had on his dress uniform and Becka thought he had never looked so handsome, with the rows of combat ribbons and the flyer's wings on his chest. Then, as the wedding party assembled, the ceremony began.

Knowing how much her sister would have loved to be there, Lou looked at the young couple and tears began to stream down her cheeks. In 1912 Lou and her husband Walter had attended Liz and Ben's wedding, having traveled all the way from Arizona to Kentucky to be present. It had been held in the home of their eldest sister, Cora, and now seemed like such a short time ago...yet here in front of her was her sister's youngest daughter…getting married!

Lou tried to listen to the old, familiar, yet meaningful words of the ceremony but her mind kept drifting back to her childhood, to the fun and adventures she and Liz had had together as children. Lou had been delighted when Becka called to tell her about their plans to be married in Phoenix…so that Becka could be with her "favorite" Aunt. She'd wanted at least some of her family to be present, and loved her Aunt Lou, so, she felt Lou would be happy to stand in for her mother…and she was right.

During the ceremony Red placed the ring on Becka's finger. The Minister then removed his long scarf and gently wrapped it around their hands as they repeated the vows. Becka noticed that Lou was weeping quietly, and her own eyes were moist. She looked at Red and saw that he, too, had moist eyes. He seemed very nervous, and ill at ease.

When the minister reached the part in the ceremony where he asked, "if anyone has cause to object to the marriage" they both jumped when a loud squeak came from the large double doors in the rear of the chapel. Two children came into the room and sat down to watch the proceedings. The minister smiled and continued with the service.

Lou had planned a wedding supper for the young couple. She had made reservations at the best hotel dining room in Phoenix. She had begged Becka and Red to remain overnight, but Red had other plans. As Ben had done so many years ago, Red, too, wanted to take his bride away, and planned to travel on to Globe, Arizona for their first night as man and wife.

After the wonderful dinner, Becka and Red thanked Lou and Mary for their kind attention to all the details, and for their loving help. Becka and Lou had tears of joy in their eyes as they parted that evening.

With the war still raging on both fronts, everyone wondered when they might see each other again. During wartime everything seemed rushed, tentative, and unstable. As a result, Red and Becka had no idea where they would be living after they reached the East Coast. But, no different from thousands of other young people, they were young and in love, and full of bright hopes for their future.

The war had changed the face of the whole nation. Families were torn apart and many young men, sons, fathers, and brothers, had fallen in battle. Many were wounded, and many would never come home again. But the small wedding party was living in the moment, and any dark clouds Becka foresaw were pushed to the back of her mind.

Becka was excited and happy, and yes, a little nervous. She had never been with a man in an intimate way. She felt unsure of herself, and ignorant about the marriage bed. She prayed that Red would understand and be patient with her. What she didn't know, and what Red did not tell her until many months later, was that when their relationship first began, Red and Curly had had a conversation about her. Had she known, she would have been very angry with them both.

"Hey Red," Curly had said one evening shortly after he and Becka had gone out. "What do you think of that little Kentucky girl I brought up to your room last week?" He was referring to the time Red had deliberately gotten him drunk and he had been so ill, he couldn't escort Becka to her apartment. He knew it was a dirty trick on Red's part, but he didn't hold a grudge. Red had looked at Curly closely, wondering if he was still seeing Becka. He didn't think so, but he wasn't sure.

"Why do you ask?" Red said in his Texas drawl.

"Oh, ole Buddy," said Curly, "I know what you were

trying to do that night. It worked, I was so damn drunk that I couldn't even stagger up those freaking stairs to her apartment. You did a good job, you skunk!" Curly laughed and continued. "I had the mother of all hangovers the next day!"

Red laughed also, and said "I guess I owe you an apology, but she just seemed too sweet for a rounder like you. I knew you didn't have any good intentions."

Curly had laughed again. "Well," he said, "you were right, but I don't think it would have done me any good. She is a really nice little gal, and between us, I think she is a virgin." Curly had looked at Red for a moment longer, then said, "I may be a rounder, but I'm not in the habit of 'de-flowering' young innocent girls."

Red had felt a lift to his spirits as he listened to Curly. He was drawn to Becka as he had never been drawn to any other girl. He felt a strong attraction to her, and wanted to see her as much as possible. They seemed to have a special chemistry that was unique to him. He didn't understand it, but he knew, even at that early stage in their relationship that he was falling in love with her. He wanted to be with her as often as possible, and had called her every day since the first time they had gone out. They had actually met on March 19th, and here they were on May 2nd, getting married!

After the delicious dinner, Becka returned to Mary's home with Aunt Lou and Mary, to shower and change for their trip. Red had gone to refuel the car. By 8 p.m. they were on their way north out of Phoenix.

When they arrived in Globe it was very late and both were tired. Red had reserved a nice room in a large motel. In their room was a coffee maker and before long, Becka had coffee brewing. She had found some English shortbread cookies to go with the coffee. Both showered and put on large white robes that were furnished by the motel, then sat at the small round table and drank coffee and ate the cookies.

As Red looked at Becka across the small table, his heart filled with love and desire for her. Becka was returning his look of affection and love. She was still a little nervous, but her feelings for this man were deep and exciting. She looked at his chiseled features, his deep blue eyes, his square, strong chin, and the tousled red hair. She knew that she loved him more than life itself!

Red stood up and came around the table. He gently lifted Becka in his arms and carried her to the large bed. Slipping off her robe, he marveled at her creamy skin and the way her dark hair fell around her shoulders. He felt her tremble as he pulled back the covers and slipped her in the bed. He reached over and turned off the lights, and dropping his own robe beside the bed, he slipped in next to Becka.

She soon discovered that she had no reason to be nervous or uncomfortable. Red was gentle, playful, and had all the skills needed to make Becka feel loved and desired. They fell asleep that night in each other's arms, and awoke late the next morning to a glorious day of bright sunshine. After showering and dressing they walked down to the small town of Globe. They found a café and ordered breakfast.

Red was looking at Becka across the table with such intensity that she laughed.

"What?" she demanded.

"Do you know that I'd like to take you back to the room and get back in bed?" Red said with a twinkle in his eyes.

"Why not?" laughed Becka, "After all, wc are on our honeymoon!"

They finally left Globe by 2 P.M..... checkout time.

Their journey across the United States from California to North Carolina was glorious, exciting and fun. They spent the time in the car talking about themselves, their families, their hobbies, and their beliefs, and getting to know each other better and better.

They had stopped in Midland, Texas and found Red's grandmother. She seemed delighted to meet Becka and made her feel comfortable and welcome. Memo, the name Red used for his grandmother, was a very nice looking woman. She was surprisingly young looking for a grandmother with a grandson as old as Red. They went out to eat together, and had a very nice visit.

As they traveled on, Becka was much more open about herself. Red, however, remained reticent and seemed to keep some things about his life to himself. Becka sensed there were things he did not want to talk about, so she did not press him. It could wait. They had ten days before Red was to report for duty at the Cherry Point Air Base. With the optimism of youth they did not worry that they might have trouble finding a place to live.

They visited Carlsbad Caverns and other interesting sights along the way. In both Red and Becka's opinion, however, the most beautiful place they visited on the trip was Lover's Leap in Tennessee. The area was covered with tall magnificent trees, bubbling streams, and flowers and birds were everywhere! When they reached the summit and the "leap," Red remarked that they had already made their leap. He pulled Becka into his arms and whispered to her, feeling her sweetness and the fragrance of her cologne. "Darling, I'm so glad we made that leap," and he kissed her until she was breathless!

When they reached Cherry Point they had four days to look for an apartment. Some of Red's friends at the squadron were living in a large beach house not far from the base. There was an extra bedroom, and Red and Becka were delighted to find it.

They shared the large old frame house with three other couples, all in the Marine Air Corps. They shared the kitchen and baths and all got along famously. Becka made friends quickly with other wives and became popular for her talent to cook delicious meals.

One evening about a week after they had moved into the beach house, Red came home early. He was very upset, and asked Becka to come into their room. When they were inside the room, he shut the door and sat on the bed. He covered his face with his hands and his shoulders began to shake.

"Oh honey," Becka exclaimed, "what's the matter?"

"It's Tex, he's, he's dead!" Red said in a choking whisper. Becka gave a small cry and sank down on the bed, weeping.

"He was flying…he wasn't cleared for flying, you know," Red continued in a choked voice. "Somehow he got the plane into a reverse spin and went into a mountain…the plane didn't burn. They recovered his body, and they're sending it back to Texas, where his folks live."

Becka moved into Red's arms, and there they sat…on the bed…just holding each other.

Presently someone knocked softly at the door. Becka went to open it. Their friends had heard the news also, and wanted to know if there was anything they could do. Still numb, Becka simply shook her head. Her friend, Jill, handed Becka a thermos of coffee, two cups, napkins and some sweet rolls, then quietly closed the door and left them alone.

It took Red and Becka a long time to recover from their grief. However, Red had to return to duty, and Becka tried to resume her life. She had called Tex's parents to give them their love and prayers. She wished there was more she could do. She kept picturing Tex's happy face as he helped them load the car the day they left Laguna Beach. She could hear his voice, and his laughter in her mind, and would start crying again. The other wives at the house tried to cheer Becka up. They coaxed her to come to the beach, and sunbath with them. And, gradually, Becka resumed her place in the household. But, her heart was often heavy whenever she thought of the loss of their dear friend.

There was a water tower near the old beach house, and when the girls were not sun bathing on the beach, they climbed to the top of the tower by way of a metal ladder attached to the side. They wrapped themselves in large beach blankets and spread them out on the top of the tower where they sun bathed "in the all-together." They were happy to be getting an "all over" tan, but the four lovely nude bodies of the young women stretched out on the top of the tower was just too much for the young flyers who began swooping in low over the girls. Soon the sun bathing in the "all-together" had to be abandoned!

The four young couples enjoyed going out for dinner at the B.O.Q. and dancing at the planned entertainment on the base. Becka called her parents often and kept them aware of the happenings in and around the area where she and Red lived. She did not, however, tell her mother about the nude sunbathing. She didn't think her mother would approve!

About two months after Red and Becka moved into the old beach house, Liz called one day to give her the news from home. Liz told Becka that George, the neighbor boy, had been home on furlough. Scheduled to go back to the South Pacific for active duty, he had been over to their house for a visit and asked about Becka, Harry and Henry.

"He was surprised to hear that you were married." Liz said. "He is engaged also, and they plan to marry before he returns to active duty."

"Where is she from?" asked Becka.

"He didn't say where he met her, but her folks live in Florida."

"By the way, Mom," said Becka, changing the subject. "I think I'm going to make you a grandma!"

"Oh honey, are you sure?" exclaimed Liz.

"Yes, Mom, I'm pretty sure. I haven't told Red yet, but he's taking me to the doctor on Saturday, and then I can tell him he's going to be a daddy!" Becka laughed.

She was very excited about having a child. She also knew that Red would be just as happy as she was. They had not taken any precautions to keep from getting pregnant, and had talked a great deal about having children. Becka was already picking out names. On Saturday, when Red took her to the base doctor, her pregnancy was confirmed and both she and Red were very excited. They went straight to a local Sears store and bought all kinds of baby things!

All along, they had kept looking for a house to rent, and were fortunate to find a nice little place in a nearby town. It was furnished and Becka was delighted with it. The neighbors owned the house and were so good to Becka and Red. Every few days Becka would find fresh vegetables, corn, tomatoes, green beans, onions, watermelon and squash on the back porch. Red was delighted to have some great dinners when he arrived home after flying all day. Becka kept the small house as neat as a pin and enjoyed visiting with the elderly neighbors.

Her mother and dad had written that they were planning to come down to visit so they could meet their new son-in-law. They were coming on the train, and planned to arrive on Saturday. It was pouring the rain the day they arrived at the station where they were to transfer to the bus that would take them to La Grange where Becka and Red lived. They had to walk almost two blocks in the rain to catch the bus. Ben was lugging the suitcases, filled with Pyrex dinnerware for Becka as a wedding gift. They were soaking wet and as they boarded the bus the suitcase slipped out of Ben's grip and Liz heard the sound of broken dishes!

"Oh No! Not the dishes!" exclaimed Liz. Sure enough, most of them were cracked or broken beyond repair. A few survived – the large covered baking dish, the pie pan, and a couple of measuring cups, but all else had to be trashed.

When Ben and Liz arrived at the small home, Liz was sure Becka and Red would think they looked like a couple of drowned pack rats! Their clothes were soaked, their hair plastered to their heads, and they carried a suitcase full of broken dishes! Oh Heavens thought Liz, what an impression we must be making for our new son-in-law!

"Oh Mom, why didn't you call us when you reached the station? We could have come to pick you up. Just look at you. You will both catch your death in those wet things." And Becka hurried them back to the small guest room where they could get out of the wet things and into dry clothes.

In the meantime, she hurried to get dinner on the table. She had planned fried chicken, potatoes, green beans, fresh tomatoes, and home made biscuits. Knowing what her folks liked to eat, she had also baked an apple pie from Liz's own recipe. Red helped her set the table, and told Becka his stomach was growling, he was so hungry!

The elderly neighbors had been invited, and came in carrying fresh flowers and a chocolate cake. When all the introductions had been made, they gathered around the large oval table and Becka served the dinner. Becka was to remember her parent's visit to North Carolina and their little frame home in LaGrange as one of the happiest times of their young marriage.

During their three day visit, Ben and Liz developed an immediate fondness for Red, and the feeling was mutual for Red as well. At the end of the stay Red took them directly back to the train station, skipping the bus trip, then saw them off before he had to return to the base. The gasoline shortage made it impossible for Becka to go along, so she had to bid her parents goodbye at the house. It would have been a long round trip drive for Red if Becka had accompanied them. After they left, Becka had a good cry. It seemed that she cried much too easily now that she was expecting a baby.

Red did not try to keep anything from Becka, even if he sometimes wanted to spare her worry and pain. He had told her recently that he had been assigned to night flying school and would probably be transferring to Florida soon. They had discussed the wisdom of Becka going back home to be with her parents when the baby was due, and her parents agreed, saying it would be a prudent arrangement, considering the turmoil and unstable conditions.

The war was still raging in Europe and the Pacific, and all of them knew that Red would be sent back into combat as soon as the night fighter training was completed. The baby was expected in late February or early March. The young couple decided to take advantage of Red's 10-day leave in December and go to Kentucky for Christmas, and Becka would stay there until the baby was born. It was certain now, Red was being transferred to the night fighter unit in Florida shortly after the first of the year.

By early October the fall colors had arrived in North Carolina. The weather was crisp and there was a beautiful harvest moon. Becka got into the spirit of Halloween and decorated the little house with orange pumpkins and made pumpkin pies and delicious cup cakes and cookies for all the little "goblins" that would be knocking at their door. They invited some of their friends from the squadron for dinner and Halloween fun. The neighborhood children came in droves, enjoying the cookies and hot chocolate Becka provided. A costume party started about 8 p.m. after all the "goblins" had gone home to bed.

Not to be left out, Red's squadron buddies showed up in all kinds of crazy outfits. One couple came as Hitler and Eva Braun, and were thoroughly booed and placed in fake handcuffs and put into "prison!" They played silly games such as "spin the bottle" and "jump the bridge." But for the most part they just talked, laughed and discussed future plans.

It was a fun evening, and everyone went home feeling happy. It turned out to be a goodbye party, for most of the men were to be transferred soon. Some, as Red, would go to Florida; but others would be going back into combat. Their partings that night were bittersweet.

On the 20th of December, Becka and Red packed up all their belongings, said a fond farewell to their wonderful neighbors, and headed for Kentucky. The weather promised to be a little tricky on the automobile trip because a big snowfall was predicted between North Carolina and Kentucky. Some of the highways were over dangerous mountains, and Red was not looking forward to driving in blinding snow. He grew up in Midland, Texas where snows were very light and did not last long. Becka, however, was used to winter snows, and seemed unconcerned. Even so, Red purchased chains for the little blue Ford and hoped for the best. And a good thing, for blinding snow with fierce winds hit them near Bluefield,Virginia, forcing them to find a motel for the night.

They arrived at Becka's parents' home late on the 23rd of December. Liz had the house decorated for Christmas, Ben had a roaring fire in the fireplace, and delicious aromas came wafting from the kitchen. Red was delighted to see the home where Becka was born. He had great respect for Ben and Liz and the feelings were mutual. Red felt very comfortable and at ease with Becka's family.

After a delicious meal, he and Ben retired to the living room, while Becka and Liz laughed and cleared the dishes and tidied the kitchen. Ben asked Red about his family in Texas. Red told him briefly about his home on the dairy farm, his grandmother and his college days in Illinois.

"I grew up with a longing for a big family. I guess I was a pretty lonely little boy." He laughed, and continued, "You see, my Dad died when I was very young and my Mother got a job in a hospital. It was my grandmother who raised me. She took me to live with her on the dairy until I was grown."

Red also told Ben about his moving to Illinois and attending the University there. He said he had always wanted to fly, and was taking flying lessons the summer of 1941. He decided to join the military and become a flyer. He felt that the country would soon be in the war, and he had an opportunity to go in as an officer, and to become a fighter pilot.

"Hmm," Ben nodded "So you were already in the service when Pearl Harbor was attacked." He said it as a statement, not as a question.

Red nodded and remarked, "Yes, I was lucky to already be in the service and in training as a pilot. But the event changed all our lives."

The attack on Pearl had affected the entire world. Somewhere in the back of his mind, Red realized the great dangers ahead. The urgency of the situation and the rush to get men trained for combat was evident to all of the men in his squadron. Men, ships, planes, other military necessities, Red knew the terrible potential for loss was enormous. He had been very young in 1941, but now, well after his tour in combat (and the things he'd seen in combat) he felt like an old man. No, he had no illusions about the war...about combat...and he knew he'd be returning to combat again...back to the Pacific.

Ben realized the situation too, especially insofar as it effected his little girl. His little girl...married, and now expecting. The two now spoke quietly for a long time, Red voicing his concerns, and Ben ssuring him that Becka would be properly cared for until he returned. Red felt good about Becka being home with her parents to await the birth of their first child.

That first Christmas Red and Becka spent with her parents in Kentucky was a festive one. The weather obliged by sending a beautiful snowfall on Christmas Eve. Several of Becka's friends stopped by to see her and to meet her new husband. Aunt Lou had written a beautiful article for the local paper with Becka's picture describing the wedding. Her friends, having read the article, wanted to meet Red. Most of them were a little in awe of Red and his experiences as a fighter pilot. Many of Becka's friends had boyfriends, brothers, and a few had husbands, serving in the military.

Becka was happy to see them all, and delighted that several had brought gifts for the expected baby. Becka's friends had crocheted blankets, booties, caps, and sweaters, and she proudly displayed them. The girls had a delightful time trying to pick names for a boy or girl. However, they were all sure it was going to be a boy!

Harry surprised the family by coming home on Christmas Day. He had managed to get leave for a much-needed rest, and it was a wonderful surprise to the whole family when he walked in.

Liz and Ben could hardly believe their eyes. They had not seen their son since he left for the Navy and the battlefront. Harry had lost his youthful appearance. There were lines around his mouth and eyes. He was no longer the excited youth that left their home in January of 1942. He had matured into a competent young man who had had his share of combat, and endured many terrible hours of duty.

There was an almost instant bond between Harry and Red. The two men liked and respected each other, immediately. Harry, who had always loved and kept a special place in his heart for his little sister, felt very good about her choice of a husband.

But Harry was still Harry, and he loved to tease.

"Hey, Sis" he called as she came into the room where he and Red were talking "How come you didn't wait? I told you I had a great guy picked out for you." He said with a wink at Red. "But no, you just couldn't wait."

"Well, big brother" answered Becka, ruffling Harry's blond curls, "you were just too slow, and you know how impatient I can be."

They all laughed and Becka sat down on the arm of Harry's chair. The three young people continued to talk, but only about the lighter and more humorous aspects of the war. They talked of things such as goofs, and terrible chow, clothes that didn't fit, outrageous commanders, and so on. Presently Liz called them into the kitchen for apple pie and coffee.

Red could not remember when he had had such a wonderful, though bittersweet Christmas. It was wonderful to be with this large happy family, and bittersweet that he would have to leave shortly after Christmas to return to

Florida and night fighter training. Both Red and Harry were scheduled to leave on the 27th.

On the morning of the 26th, as soon as breakfast was over, Harry and Becka asked Red to go with them for a walk through the snowy countryside. They explained to Red that it was one of their favorite things to do. Red readily agreed, and the three set off for a long crisp walk. They bundled up with boots, borrowed boots for Red, plus a borrowed overcoat — he had neither and was not prepared for this kind of weather.

He was grateful for the extra layer of clothing, as it was quite cold, with a smart wind blowing down from the north. Their breath made white puffs and their ears turned red from the wind. Red pulled the scarf around his head and Harry and Becka pulled their caps down over their ears. They walked the old trail, over the footpath, and the bridge across the frozen creek. Becka told Red about her experience of having her big toe in the pinchers of a bad-tempered crawdad. She and Harry laughed, remembering that day and how Johnny, their sister Maggie's boyfriend had removed the crawdad.

They reached the hill overlooking the mighty Ohio River. It could be seen plainly in the distance, as most of the trees were bare of leaves at this time of year. The view was beautiful with the sun sparkling on the new fallen snow, the hedgerows and fir trees covered with white snow garments. Slow moving barges were making their way down the river, heading toward the Mississippi River and beyond.

"It's really lovely here," said Red "but I'd have to get used to this weather. It didn't snow much in Texas, and I never did learn to drive in this climate." He continued, his words coming out with white puffs from the cold. "When Becka and I drove up from North Carolina, I was very nervous driving through those mountains in Virginia during that near blizzard!"

Harry laughed. "Well," he said to Red, "don't be ashamed of that. We all feel a little nervous driving in this kind of weather."

"Look!" said Becka, "there are ice flows on the river. I just didn't realize how cold it really is!"

When the three returned to the house, Liz had fresh coffee and pumpkin pie, Christmas cookies, nuts and candies waiting for them. They removed their heavy boots and coats and went into the living room where a warm blazing fire welcomed them. Liz brought a tray of coffee, pie and cookies and other delights. The Christmas tree twinkled and soft Christmas carols played from the radio. It was a day that they were all to remember and cherish. Harry and Red would think of this wonderful day again and again as they lay in their bunks far away, Red in the South Pacific, and Harry on the great battleship as it engaged the Japanese in combat.

"This is one of the best Christmases I've ever known," said Red to no one in particular. "We never had a Christmas tree when I was a little boy. Oh, we got gifts on Christmas morning, but it was just another day of milking cows, preparing the milk, and driving it into town."

He told them about the Christmas morning when he found a beautiful pony outside his bedroom window. Liz and Ben, as well as Becka and Harry were listening intently to Red's description of his childhood remembrances.

Red looked around, embarrassed, "I'm sorry" he said, "I seem to be doing all the talking."

"Hey," said Harry quickly, "Not everyone celebrates Christmas the same way. Mom and Dad here always made a big thing of it…for us kids, you know," and he laughed and put an arm around his mother.

"Yeah," said Becka. "Remember the time Daddy played Santa?" And both Becka and Harry laughed.

Ben cleared his throat and said in a very deep voice "I think I made a pretty good Santa, Ho! Ho! Ho!" he stood up and went over to the fireplace, He put another log on the fire and looked at Becka with twinkling eyes. "I know a cute little five year old who was surprised to get a pretty little red sled!" He crossed the room and gave Becka a hug. "Too bad it didn't snow for Christmas. I tell you Red, this little girl gave us a hard time until it finally did snow!" Everyone laughed, Liz, Ben and Harry remembering, and Red picturing little Becka worrying everyone about the "no snow show."

All too quickly the day came for the men to leave for duty. Becka tried her best to be brave, but it was very difficult — she and Red had not been apart since their marriage. She swallowed her tears and kissed him goodbye before he left. As she did, he promised that if it were at all possible, he would get a short leave to come back in time for the baby's birth.

The baby made her appearance on Sunday, February 19, 1945. Red did indeed get a few days' leave and was at the hospital the day his little daughter was born. He slipped into the hospital room and bent down and kissed Becka's cheek. She was very tired but so happy to see him.

"Have you seen her?" she asked. "She is so beautiful, She has red hair, like you! The door opened and a white clad nurse came quietly into the room. She placed the small bundle next to Becka.

"Please," Becka said quietly to the nurse "Give her to her Daddy, just for a few minutes."

The nurse smiled and placed the tiny bundle into Red's arms. He held her as though she might break into a million pieces. He quickly sat down and looked at the tiny red face, the strawberry blonde hair, and touched her tiny little hand. The baby's fingers closed around his big thumb, She seemed to be looking at him with curiosity.

"Oh, My God!" was all Red could manage. He gently hugged the tiny child. "Oh My God," he said again, as though it was a prayer.

"Well, Daddy," Becka said to Red with a trace of her old mischief. "You were so sure it was going to be a boy. Now what are we going to name our new little "Leatherneck?"

Both Red and Becka were smiling, remembering the very cute announcements that Harry had made for them. He had printed about 50 of them to send to relatives and friends. The announcements had a hand drawn picture of a little boy holding a Marine officer's cap, with a poem on the inside of the card that read.

> "Leathernecks! Look to your laurels! A new boot is wearing the green! Becka and Red proudly present the world's very youngest Marine!"

"Well, Mama" Red said in his Texas drawl "I think we should use the announcements just the way they are. Our little red-head here may make a great Marine someday."

"I agree," said Becka. "Shall we call her Sharon Lee?"

"Sure" agreed Red. "That's a beautiful name for such a beautiful little lady.

Red felt so happy and proud of his wife and little daughter. When he returned to the Air Station at Vero Beach, Florida, he treated all his flying buddies to Havana cigars, and all the secretaries and civilian personnel to boxes of chocolates. He knew that he would be in training for several more months and wanted his wife and child there with him. He began to look for a place for them to live.

As always in war time, rentals were few and far between. However, he did find a place in a small town called Sebastian, near Vero Beach. It was a nice room and bath with kitchen privileges, in the home of a very nice lady. Mrs. Roundtree was gracious and happy to have them. Red called Becka right away to tell her the good news.

Little Sherry was two and a half months old, and doing fine. Becka and Sherry left Ashland in mid-April and took the train to Vero Beach, Florida. Red met them at the station and they quickly settled into the lovely old beach home. It had a wide veranda on the front with large windows and their room was spacious and comfortable. The baby slept in her large buggy and the buggy was convenient to take her for walks and outings during the day.

Sebastian was close to the Indian River and Mrs. Roundtree took a long canoe out several days each week. She was quite a fisherwoman, for she seldom came home empty handed. She caught large rainbow trout, and they were delicious the way Becka prepared them. Mrs. Roundtree had a crippled leg and walked with a crutch, but she never complained, and always seemed in good humor. She enjoyed Becka's cooking, and Becka often did the cooking while "Roundie" as she was nicknamed, held and played with little Sherry.

There was an old Maytag ringer washing machine on the back porch where Becka washed the baby's many diapers and hung them on the line to dry. She and Red were very happy there in that beautiful beach home. When time permitted they went out to dinner or to the officer's club for dances and parties. Mrs. Roundtree, who did not have any children of her own, delighted in looking after little Sherry when the young couple went out.

This was seldom, because of Red's intensive night fighter training. He flew at night, and had to sleep during the day. It was often very warm and humid during the day and he had trouble sleeping. When he arrived at the Base at eleven thirty each night, he drank coffee and was served scrambled eggs. When he got off duty the next morning, he drank coffee and was served scrambled eggs…and lost a lot of weight. His normal weight was about 200 pounds and he dropped to about 160 in the few months they were in Florida. The flight surgeon was concerned and ordered Red to "eat more steaks."

Becka tried to get Red to eat more, but he just wasn't hungry! She began encouraging Red to have ice cream and cookies with his coffee before he left for the Base. And when he came home the next morning she tempted him with cinnamon rolls and milk before he slept. She suggested that he not have coffee in the mornings, but ask for milk instead. Red gradually gained a little of he weight but remained on the slim side, weighing only about 170 pounds.

Early one Monday morning, before Red was home from his night flights, Becka was hanging a fresh load of diapers on the line. Suddenly she heard a roar overhead, and a fighter plane swooped low over the house "flat-hating." Both Becka and Mrs. Roundtree looked up at the plane. It seemed to be no more than one hundred feet above them.

Mrs. Roundtree laughed. "That's your Captain, honey, and he's saluting you!"

In a few minutes the plane came roaring back, wagging its wings when it came over the house. Becka grabbed a diaper and waved it back and forth, hoping that the pilot could see her. She didn't quite believe it was Red. He was usually careful to obey all the rules. And this was certainly against the rules! When he got home that morning she asked him if he'd done a little "flat hating" lately. He grinned and hugged her.

"Hey," she said, "you know you're not supposed to do that. But I loved it, anyway!"

Red laughed and picked up little Sherry, holding her up in the air over his head. Sherry kicked her chubby legs and giggled. The baby was growing so fast and changing so much it was hard to realize she was only four months old. She was sitting alone, now, drinking from a cup and holding toys in her hands. She already had four teeth, and Becka didn't know how much longer she would be able to nurse her.

In early June, Red told Becka that his squadron would be leaving soon for combat duty in the Pacific. Becka's heart sank. She just didn't know how she could stand to part from him and know he was going into combat. She prayed that the Lord would give her the strength to let him go gracefully.

Red was given a ten-day leave before he was to report to the West Coast and join his squadron. He was promoted to Major, and would be the squadron's executive officer. It seemed to Becka that their time together in that lovely little town of Sebastian, Florida, had been all too short. They packed their few belongings, hugged and kissed Roundie and headed for Kentucky.

The baby loved riding in the car, and was a fine little traveler. Liz and Ben were expecting them when they arrived at their home in Westfield, just outside of Ashland. Liz and Ben had the front room ready for them, with a crib and playpen, and even a highchair for little Sherry. Red looked around in appreciation. He felt confident that Becka would be in fine hands while he was away. But, Oh God, how he hated to leave them!

Red could only spend a couple of days in Kentucky before he had to leave. Tears streamed down Becka's face the morning Red had to leave. Liz was crying as well, and Ben had moist eyes. As Red hugged Becka and his little daughter, tears were running down his face.

He drove his car to the West Coast and sold it although much later, he would regret that sale — cars were hard to find in the post-war months. But within a few weeks Red was back in combat in the islands of the South Pacific.

The Pacific war was fierce and intense. His squadron was in many battles, and experienced casualties and the loss of planes. Red was involved in the battle of the Peleliu Islands. It was a horrendous fight, with over 17,000 men killed on both sides.

Red's letters to Becka were few and said little of what he was experiencing. In his letters he described the beautiful beaches and his hunt for shells and "snake eyes" which were small stone-like solid oval shells that resembled snakes' eyes. He managed to send enough beautiful small shells to Becka that she had them made into buttons and sewn on a new gold tone suit.

Many years later, Red and Becka took a trip to the South Pacific Islands where Red had been stationed and involved in the terrible war with the Japanese. He wanted Becka to see those lovely Islands and to visit those places with him. At the time of their visit to the Islands, 35 years had passed and the Islands had recovered their original beauty.

Red's eyes were moist remembering how the forests and landscape had been destroyed by the war. He was even able to find the native man who had become his friend during the time he was on one of the Islands. His friend, Bill Kane (pronounced Kahnay) was very happy to see him again.

Red and Becka visited the tiny island of Pele where Bill lived. They were treated like visiting royalty! On this same trip they visited Tokyo, Japan, and in China where they walked on the Great Wall and visited the ancient cities. Included in this six week vacation was a visit to Australia, and cities where Red had gone for R and R during his tour of duty in the South Pacific Islands. The trip was to be the highlight of their memories of the war years).

In the early summer months of 1945, the news of the Pacific war was not good. The U.S. was now bombing the main islands of Japan with seemingly little affect on the progress of the war. President Roosevelt's death had caused great turmoil in the political arena, however, the new president, Harry Truman was proving to be quite capable of filling the enormous shoes of F.D.R. Liz and Ben followed the news carefully, and prayed daily for the new President, as well as for a speedy victory for all the allies.

Their prayers and those of many others were answered as far as Europe was concerned. The war there had finally ended with an allied victory, and now the U.S. would be better able to concentrate on the war in the Pacific. Best of all, however, Henry would be coming home soon!

After the end of the war in Europe, the Becka and little Sherry were very comfortable living with Liz and Ben. Liz had furnished the front bedroom with all the things needed for both Mama and baby. Becka was unable to do much visiting, as Ben still worked at the Mill and they had only one car. However she did have friends who came to visit, and sometimes they took her to shop and for outings in the local parks.

Little Sherry was growing fast and already beginning to say many words. She was a lovely child, with big blue eyes, soft red gold hair and a sweet, lovable nature. Becka sent Red many pictures of the baby and described all the things they were doing. Ben was working only the day shift now. He showered each afternoon at the mill and put on clean clothes, and was home each evening by five o'clock. And, without fail, Liz and Becka would always have a delicious supper waiting for him.

Becka and Ben had many long talks together. Becka felt that she had never been as close to her parents — especially her Dad — during those months she lived with them waiting for Red to return.

Ben loved to play with the baby, and would take her on his lap and swing with her on the front porch. He enjoyed this time together with little Sherry, while Becka and Liz set the table and finished the dinner preparations. As always, Liz had delicious meals prepared. Fried or baked chicken, fresh vegetables, hot biscuits, potatoes and gravy, and of course, apple pie or lemon custard, and sometimes butterscotch pie, Becka's favorite.

Then the war in the Pacific ended!

On August 6th and August 9th, two atomic bombs were dropped on two different cities in Japan. V.J. day came on August 14th. V.J. Victory over Japan!

However, Red was unable to come home right away, but he was able to finally make it home before Christmas. Sherry was ten months old, walking, saying many words, and getting into all sorts of things. Red couldn't believe how much she had grown! Sherry was shy of him, at first, but soon warmed up to her Daddy, and they bonded all over again.

Becka and Liz had a beautiful Christmas tree in the living room. They placed it in front of the large window that faced the street. Liz had many ornaments saved over the years, including the ones made by the twins, Harry and Henry. It was Sherry's first Christmas. The lights and the ornaments enchanted her. She managed to overturn the tree twice, before Ben put the tree inside the playpen so that her little hands couldn't reach the branches. She would toddle up to the tree, peer through the bars of the playpen, and reach in as far as her little arms would allow. She called Liz "Nanny" and would cry: "Nanny, Nanny, Sherry pretty balls!" She loved to ride in the car, and would say, "Go bye bye in car car" when Ben came home from work.

There were no seat belts or baby seats in cars in those days, and Ben could not take her unless Becka or Liz came along to hold her. That summer before the war ended, Ben and Liz with Becka and Sherry sometimes took drives into the country on Saturdays or Sundays. They drove out to see Beulah, who lived on a large farm where she had moved after her husband's death. She worked for the folks who owned the farm, and Ben and Liz who were friends of these folks, were always welcome visitors. Beulah and Becka would take little Sherry to see the horses and cows, the chickens and of course, the many cats, kittens, and puppies.

On these occasions Beulah and Becka would have long talks. Beulah often asked Becka about her dreams. Beulah had been such a comfort to Becka during her childhood and teen-age years. Becka trusted Beulah completely, and always confided in her. Beulah had grown older and was showing her age. Her face had deep wrinkles around her eyes and mouth, and her black curly hair was almost white. The things that Bart had taught her had helped her in many ways. She was able to keep the household accounts for the Kincaid's, the folks where she lived. She was active in her church, and often taught Sunday school classes.

That first Christmas after Red came home was very special. He stayed in the Reserves, but was able to wear civilian clothes. He looked so different in "civvies." Becka and Red had fun shopping for his new "duds." Becka soon found out that Red didn't want anyone else to buy clothes for him. He was very particular and wanted to buy his own clothes. His grandmother, Memo, sent him several yards of a beautiful wool blend material for a new suit. He had it tailor-made and he looked absolutely "knock down" handsome in it!

Red and Becka were very appreciative of Ben and Liz's hospitality. However, soon after Red's homecoming, he wanted to look for their own place, and they talked about moving back to California. The young couple had some money saved, and Ben suggested that they build their own place. He offered them a nice 70 by 100 foot lot on the east portion of his property facing Wheatly Road. Red and Becka talked this over, and although Becka was not really sure this was the best thing for them, (she really wanted to move back to California), they decided to take their savings and build their own home here in Westview.

With much help from Ben, who knew all about carpentry, electric wiring and plumbing, the house began to take shape. Red told Becka that he was an excellent "gofer." He said Ben had him "gofer this and gofer that" but he was happy to do anything he could. The building process did not go well, however, because of the limited supply of materials after the war. They had difficulty obtaining nails, plumbing supplies, electrical wiring and other very necessary items.

They moved into the house before it was quite finished. It was livable, but unpainted inside, lacking many necessary things. In 1946 the winter months proved to be bitter cold, with one snowfall after another during October, November and December. Red had used most of the savings building the house, and although it was still not finished, he felt he must get a job soon. It was his intention to become a Certified Public Accountant. Getting the training and finding a job proved to be very difficult. He didn't have a car, and kicked himself for selling that sweet little blue Ford.

"I should have listened to you, Becka," he said. "You wanted me to keep it, I know. And you were so right!"

Cars were a premium, and Red finally located a used Chevy, not in the best shape, for it had been used as a taxicab. However, the price was right, so he bought it. Ben looked it over, examined the motor and brakes, the transmission and wiring, and found it to be sound in those areas. However, the upholstery was very used and worn.

The acquisition of a car freed Red to attend the college classes and look for work with much more freedom. The only job he could find was a position in a local bank, paying only 140 dollars per month! They were rapidly running out of money, and Red did not want Becka to go to work. Ben and Liz offered to help, but Red was against taking any more help from his in-laws. He felt they had been more than generous, with the gift of property and Ben's excellent help in building the two-story home. The house was very livable even if not completely finished.

After the terrible winter, Becka began to dream of California. She had voiced her doubts about building in Westfield and really wanted to return to California, but Ben and Liz had made the offer of property and Red felt they had sufficient funds to build a nice home there. Neither Becka nor Red realized how difficult it would be to obtain building materials, buy a car, or find suitable work. The post-war brought many shortages of almost everything needed to build, repair, or replace.

One evening after dinner, Liz said to Ben, "I don't think Becka is very happy, honey."

"Why do you say that?" Ben asked.

"Well, I really don't think she ever wanted to stay here, I mean make their permanent home here." And Liz shook her head sadly.

"You may be right, Liz," said Ben thoughtfully. "They both loved California; maybe we shouldn't have encouraged them to remain here."

"Oh Ben" cried Liz "I do so want them to like it here, and stay. I will be broken-hearted if they move, and I think they are considering it."

"Well, sweetheart, we must let them do what they think best. We can't stand in their way, or make them feel guilty about moving." Ben put his arms around Liz and gave her a hug and a kiss. "We'll just have to show brave faces, and give them moral support and love, even if we feel sad about the possibility of their leaving.

"Maybe they won't leave, honey. Maybe Red will find a good paying job." Ben added this hopefully, but in his heart he knew that Becka and Red would probably move back to California, if not right away, then soon.

And Ben was right in his prediction. Within a year, Becka and Red had sold the house, for a nice profit. They insisted on Ben and Liz taking a portion of the sale, enough to cover the cost of the lot, and Becka gave her mother all the nice furniture she had purchased. She didn't need it because Red had purchased a house trailer. He'd rigged the Chevy with a trailer hitch and stronger springs, so they could pull their little "covered wagon" across the "plains" to California!

They watched the weather reports, and picked a week that was predicted to be "mild" across the country, and pulled out of the driveway early one morning in January of 1947. Little Sherry was almost 2 years old, and very active and aware of everything around her. They had installed a good car heater and made Sherry a comfortable bed and play area in the back seat of the Chevy.

The morning they left, there were many tears. Even little

Sherry seemed to know that she would not see her wonderful Nanny for a long time. Although Liz's heart was breaking, she tried to be brave. Ben offered Red extra money for the trip. Red, however, although gracious about it, refused any monetary help.

"No Ben," he said with feeling, "You and Liz have been more than kind and generous to us. We will never be able to repay you. As soon as we are settled in a place in Southern California, you and Liz must come out and spend the winter with us. Just get up and come, and leave this terrible weather for a few months with us."

Red knew that Ben was planning to retire before many more years, and would be free to spend some time in California.

"Well," drawled Ben, "we may just surprise you with a visit. In the meantime, please do write and call often. Liz is pretty broken up about your moving."

Becka would always remember looking back at her mother, standing forlornly in the driveway as they pulled out onto Bellefonte Road and headed west. Her eyes filled with tears, and she had a feeling of guilt for leaving her parents.

Red and Becka were very lucky with good weather all the way across the country. There were a few snow flurries in Tennessee and Oklahoma, but the rest of the trip was fairly mild.

Red handled the car and trailer like a pro, keeping his speed between 50 and 55 miles per hour. They found trailer parks along the way, and quickly became familiar with "trailer living." The only trouble they had came as they entered Texas. Little Sherry became ill with a fever and refused to eat. They had planned to visit with Aunt Lou in El Paso where she lived with her son Dan and his wife, Margie. They called Dan and explained the circumstances, and Dan insisted they come there immediately.

He arranged for a doctor to examine Sherry, and everyone was pleased that she was not seriously ill. The doctor said she had a bad case of motion sickness, and needed a few days rest from the constant traveling in the car. They parked the trailer in Dan's driveway and he graciously offered a guest bedroom for the young family. Becka was very glad to be able to visit with her wonderful Aunt Lou. And she had always been fond of Dan and Margie.

They had experienced a tragedy of their own a few months earlier. Margie had miscarried their first child, and they had been overcome with grief at the loss of their first tiny son. Within a few days of quiet living, Sherry regained her appetite and quickly became her old happy self.

One day during their brief stay with Dan, Margie and Aunt Lou, they all drove down to Mexico, which was not far from Dan's home. Dan purchased a hand made jacket for little Sherry. Sherry would keep the jacket the rest of her life. Years later when she had a home of her own, she framed the tiny, beautiful, hand made jacket and hung it on her wall along with other hand made articles of baby clothing.

They once again had Sherry examined by a doctor, and after receiving a clean "bill of health," the young family left Texas and continued their drive to California. Crossing the states of New Mexico and Arizona, they arrived in El Monte, California on January 17th where they finally found a trailer park that would admit children. They had stopped at many parks but were turned away because they had a child.

The following Monday morning Red drove into Los Angeles to look for work. He found a position on the third day as an accountant for an Ice Cream Company. Although the pay was not good, he had the opportunity to advance quickly. Although Red was still adamant about Becka's not working. they soon found that living expenses required her to find a job. After some difficulty, they found a day care center for Sherry and Becka found an excellent job with the County of Los Angeles in the Juvenile Division of the Probation Office. She worked for several probation officers in the capacity of secretary and probation officer assistant. She liked the work and it paid even more than Red was making. Since they both worked in downtown L.A. they were able to drive to and from work together.

Becka hated leaving Sherry each day. Often, she cried for her Mommy and refused to eat. She could talk quite well, but didn't say a word at the day care center. When she was being put to bed one evening, she cried and suddenly said to Becka,

"They put me in the cloak room, Mama, and it's dark in there!" Becka was so upset about this that she confronted the owner of the day care center. The woman denied that she put Sherry in the closet.

"Who told you that we put her there?" she asked indignantly.

"Sherry told me, herself," answered Becka.

"How can she tell you?" asked the woman. "She can't talk. She hasn't said one word except, 'Mommy' since she's been here."

"Sherry has been talking since before she was a year old. And I believe her. I think it's terrible that you would do a thing like that to a little two year old!" Becka told the woman with anger in her voice.

"Well, you see, Mrs. Duncan," said the day care owner, "Sherry cried all the time. We had to punish her to keep her quiet." And the woman actually seemed to think that her "punishment " of the child was justified.

"I will not be bringing her back here anymore!" said

Becka and she walked out, determined to find a safer and happier place for her little daughter. One of the caretakers, a lovely black woman, followed Becka as she and the little girl left the center.

"Pardon me, Mrs. Duncan," she said, "I'm glad you're taking this child home," she said, stooping down and kissing the little girl on the top of her blond curls. "She was so unhappy here. I felt so sorry for her, and tried to console her, but she just kept crying and asking for her mommy."

Becka thanked the woman and smiled, feeling a little better, but was still angry at the treatment Sherry had received at the day care center. Back at the trailer park, the manager offered to look after Sherry until Becka was able to find a permanent sitter. Becka quickly agreed, and was soon able to make suitable arrangements. She located a nurse in the nearby community. The woman, Mrs. Hutchins, had four children of her own, and did not work. She wanted to stay home with her little family until the children were older. She fell in love with little Sherry and told Becka she would be delighted to care for her.

It was arranged, and Sherry loved her new babysitter, "Hutchie" as she called her. The fee for childcare was reasonable and things went much more smoothly for Becka and Sherry. Red was advancing in his job, and the young couple was talking about getting a home soon. However those plans were postponed when, in November of that year Becka discovered that she was expecting their second child.

She continued to work until April. She was five months pregnant and although she felt well, Red wanted her to quit work and stay home until her due date in August. By then, he had advanced in his job, and was making enough money so that Becka's leaving work would not place them in a financial bind. They found a small house nearby, and moved their house trailer into the court there and rented to a young couple with a small child.

They became the managers of the trailer court and quickly got acquainted with several of the young couples living there. One couple in particular, Vera and Andy, became good friends. Vera was also expecting a baby about the same time as Becka, and the two young women made baby clothes and enjoyed reading the newest books on baby care.

Red's grandmother planned to come to El Monte during the month of August. She wanted to help Becka and Red with caring for Sherry while Becka was busy with the new baby. Becka and Red were delighted that Memo could come, and Red sent her bus money and expenses.

The Greyhound bus stopped in El Monte and Red picked up his grandmother. She was a big help to Becka; Sherry adored her and her presence made things much smoother and easier for Becka. It had been a difficult pregnancy. The weather was very hot that summer and Becka suffered greatly from the heat. Her legs and feet swelled and she had severe headaches.

Becka and her neighbor sometimes sat on the front lawn, trying to catch a cool breeze. There was no air-conditioning in the small house or in the neighbor's trailer. One morning, the two very pregnant women were sitting talking and fanning themselves, when one of the older gentlemen living in the trailer park came walking past. He stopped and looked at the two young women.

"Don't worry, girls," he said, "you'll soon be back to your girlish figures, but I'll still have my big belly!" He patted his large belly and winked at the girls.

Both of them laughed, looking at the gentleman's large, very protruding front!

Becka had a long hard labor, lasting on and off over two days. The doctor was afraid that it would be necessary to perform a C-Section. However, Becka was able to have a normal delivery. The beautiful little dark haired boy was born on Saturday night, August 14th. He weighed almost 8 pounds, had blue eyes, and a lusty cry! Red had stayed at the hospital during the long labor, sleeping fitfully on a wooden bench in the waiting room. Needless to say, both Mommy and Daddy were worn out when little Davy made his appearance and was handed into his mother's waiting arms.

They had decided earlier that if the baby were a boy they would name him David Warren. They called him Davy from the beginning. He was a happy, healthy baby, seldom cried, and slept all night long right from the first day Becka brought him home from the hospital.

Little Sherry was overjoyed with this new baby. She wanted to hold him and play with him constantly. Soon he was big enough to respond to Sherry's attentions. She had a small-overstuffed rocking chair. It was bright blue and she loved to sit in it and "read" to the baby. Becka took two long dish towels, tied them together, and placed the two month old baby in Becka's arms while Sherry was sitting in the little rocker. She tied the towels around them both, being careful that they were secure and safe. Then Sherry would rock the baby and "read." The two children often fell asleep in the chair.

But things weren't always so wonderful. While living in El Monte, Sherry had been attending Kindergarten in El Monte and had given her Mother a frightening scare. She took her lunch each day and rode the school bus. One day the bus driver let her off the bus almost 10 blocks from home. (Sherry had told the bus driver she knew the way home!) When Sherry got off the bus and looked around, she didn't see her home but she did see a car lot with pennant flags hanging and waving in the wind. There was a car lot just like that near her home! She crossed the busy street, obeying the lights as her mother had taught her and walked up to the lot, but it was not the right one. There was no trailer park just around the corner. Finally, after walking several blocks, she knew she was lost! She was only 4 and one half years old. She stopped and looked for a familiar site, but found none. She went into a small hardware store, and walking up to the clerk, told him her name and said, "I think I'm lost." She showed him her name and address on her lunch box. She was solemn, but not crying. The clerk called the local police, and soon they had her in the police car and on the way home.

Becka, meanwhile, had seen the bus go by without leaving Sherry. She had called the school to find out what was going on and was told the bus driver had already returned to the school, and claimed he had left the child on the corner near her home. Becka immediately called the police, and was frantic by the time the police car pull into the driveway. She didn't see little Sherry in the car and only seeing the two policemen, thought the worst! She was overjoyed when one of the policemen opened the back door of the car and Sherry climbed out and ran toward her mother. Becka called the principal of the school and sent the police report that stated where the child had been left. The bus driver was fired, and the school sent a letter of apology to Becka and Red.

Memo had stayed with them for six weeks and left for her own home in Texas about the middle of September. Becka had grown to love Memo and was sad to see her leave. Meanwhile, Red had been looking for another job out of the Los Angeles area. He hated the heavy traffic and the smog. They wanted to move either south toward San Diego, or north toward Ventura or Santa Barbara. When Davy was about a year old, he began to develop a bad cough that didn't respond to the usual medications. They took him to a doctor and were told that he was allergic to the smog and smoke of the big city. Red increased his efforts to find work somewhere out of the Los Angeles area. Becka still dreamed of Laguna Beach, but jobs were very hard to find in that small community.

Red came home one evening and told Becka that he had been offered a job in Ventura.

"Ventura is located about 100 miles north of here. It's a beach city free of smog, and it's not crowded," Red told her.

Both Red and Becka felt that the move to Ventura would be a good thing, and the little family moved there in the fall of 1949. They decided to find a place to live that was close to the schools and not so crowded. They were unable to find anything in Ventura, but the small mountain town of Ojai had rentals and good schools. It was located about 15 miles north of Ventura and Red felt it would be a good place to begin their residency in this new area.

Becka, although disappointed that they were unable to find a residence in Ventura, loved Ojai from the first day they moved into their apartment. It was a beautiful little town, and in many ways reminded Becka of Laguna Beach. Red liked his new job and soon became office manager, but continued to look for a place nearer his work. It was a two-lane road from Ventura to Ojai and often very slow traveling, especially if a slow moving truck blocked the way.

While the school was close enough for Sherry to walk, Becka would put Davy in the stroller and walk her to school each morning, then walk her home in the afternoon (they had only one car, and Red had to drive it to work).

Sherry was enrolled in the kindergarten class and loved her teacher. (Many years later, Sherry took a position as Assistant Superintendent in the Ojai school district, and interviewed for her job in the very room where she had attended kindergarten so many years before. While the school had been remodeled, it still looked the same to Sherry)

The neighbors in their apartment complex were friendly, and the children had much fun. Becka tried to keep Davy safe by putting him in a playpen outside the apartment during the day. However, he was a strong little guy and would shake the playpen trying to climb out! He ruined three playpens before Becka and Red just gave up. There was no fence around the yard, so Becka had to keep him inside with her, or stay with him when he was outside.

They were soon able to find a small house at the beach in Ventura much nearer Red's work, and quickly rented it. One morning after Sherry had been taken to school, Becka was washing clothes and hanging them on the line. Davy was playing in the sand near the back door. Becka went inside to get another basket of wet clothes and when she returned to the back yard Davy was missing!

She frantically called for him, running to the street and to the neighbor's home. No sign of the child! Then hearing the barking of the great Collie dog that often ran loose in the neighborhood, Becka ran toward the beach and the sound of the barking. As she mounted the sand dunes she saw the dog...and Davy. He was sitting on the sand with the foaming tide just touching his little feet, and the dog — bless it's heart — was between the child and the water, not allowing him to venture any further! Becka lifted the baby in her arms and knelt down to praise the dog, giving him a great hug.

After this frightening experience, Becka and Red were even more determined to find a better place to live, and that next spring were able to purchase a new home in the small community of Montalvo, just outside Ventura. Becka and Red were thrilled to have a home of their own. Montalvo had a good school, and most of the neighbors were young couples with children. It was an ideal place to rear youngsters.

And, Becka had tried to find the Durah's, the family that Liz had known from her teaching days and whose son, Oscar Jr., Henry had rescued during the war. They had also lived in Montalvo, but Becka could not locate anyone who had their new address. She eventually learned from Henry that Oscar's injury caused him to receive a medical discharge, and that his whole family was now living near San Francisco.

Montalvo was wonderful, but the small community did have it's drawbacks. About five miles from Ventura, Becka was again isolated. There was no bus service and only one market. The P&I Market did furnish the necessities: meat, milk, and bread, but little else. With only one car, Becka found it difficult to shop for clothes, household items and so on.

Little Sherry loved the new school and was enrolled in the first grade in the fall. Their new home was only two blocks from the school and Sherry was able to walk there each morning with some older neighbor children. Both children would attend Montalvo Elementary School through the sixth grade.

Now, at four years old, Davy would often play with the neighbor children, and with their little Cocker Spaniel dog, Pauline. As pets will do, one Saturday morning Pauline squeezed under the fence and into a neighbor's yard. Davy thought it would be fun to follow the dog, but once he got his head under the fence, there he stuck! He couldn't get under, or back out! He began to squawk his head off! Hearing him, Red went to the rescue with half the neighborhood following. The rescue was accomplished, and Davy, although much peeved, had no injuries other than slight scratches and a mouth full of dirt! Red and the neighbors, however, all had a hearty laugh.

During the years Becka and Red lived in Montalvo, Becka's parents were able to drive out for extended visits. Renting a small apartment in Ventura, Ben and Liz visited Becka and Red almost every day. Ben had only recently retired from ARMCO and had an adequate pension, although not as much as he thought he would receive after over 40 years of working there. He did, however, have the supplement of Social Security, which enabled them to do some traveling.

Liz loved Becka and Red's new home. It had three bedrooms and one bath, with a large kitchen, dining room and living room. It had a large back yard with trees and many flowers. Red had fenced the back with cinder blocks. The children had a swing in the enormous walnut tree and lots of space to play. Liz loved flowers and Becka shared this love. She had planted many flowers in the yard and Liz couldn't believe they were blooming in the winter!

"I could really get used to this kind of weather," she told Becka and Red one February afternoon.

Red's Uncle "B" as Red called him, visited them one year during the Christmas season, a delightful surprise for the young family. The weather was warm and lovely at the time Uncle B visited and he really enjoyed himself, buying all sorts of great toys for the children's Christmas. His visit was all too short, as he had to return to Detroit where he worked for the Ford Motor Company.

But California offers other, less pleasant experiences. Becka was glad that none of the relatives were there to experience the earthquake that next year – 1952. Early one morning in the summer when Red was at work at the Pt. Mugu Fire Department, Becka awoke with a start. The whole house was shaking, and the doors and windows rattled violently. Becka knew immediately what it was. Earthquake! Having experienced an earthquake while working at the probation offices in Los Angeles, she immediately jumped out of bed. Grabbing Davy from his crib, she ran down the hall and into the back yard, placing him on his blanket on the dew-wet lawn, away from power lines and immediate danger. She then ran back for Sherry, carried her outside and placed her near Davy. She had accomplished this in the space of no more than 30 seconds!

But the ground was still moving. Looking up, Becka saw power lines breaking, and “hot” lines were flying around so she decided to get under a secure door frame. Davy was squalling, but hadn’t moved so she grabbed both the children and stood in the open kitchen door, holding both frightened youngsters tightly in her arms. As she quieted them and hugged them to her, it seemed to Becka that the house continued to shake for a long time. In reality, though, the quake lasted less than a minute.

After the quaking stopped, Becka soothed both youngsters and they looked around the house for damage. The closet doors had been flung open from the shaking and some of the linens, towels and blankets were scattered on the hall floor. Pots and pans that were on the kitchen range, had fallen to the floor, and some things in the cupboards were on the counters and floor in the kitchen. Luckily, however, there was no real damage.

Red, working every other day (and night) as a fireman

had experienced the shock waves of the earthquake, and was worried about his family. He tried to call, but the lines were out. It took several hours for the electric and telephone lines to be restored and by the next day all seemed in good order. There were several "after-shocks" but nothing major.

The news said the quake was a magnitude of 7.7 and was centered in Kern County on the White Wolf Fault. Occurring at 4:52 a.m., the quake was respomsible for 13 fatalities, and nearly destroyed the little town of Tehachapi in Kern County. Later, it was determined to be the largest earthquake to hit California since San Francisco was nearly destroyed in 1906.

And figuring line of sight, Montalvo was close. Becka and her family were about 80 miles from the epicenter, and as the news went out across the nation, she received many calls from nervous relatives asking if they were all right. She was pretty shaken up, but laughed and teasingly told them that the earthquake was not nearly as bad as the hurricanes and twisters back east! She fervently hoped, however, that she would not experience another like it any time soon!

Memo was able to visit while the family lived in Montalvo. Now in her mid 70s, she was active and young for her age. She joined the family in a famous "grunion hunt" at the Ventura Beach, and caught many of the little silver fish with her bare hands. She cleaned them and cooked them for dinner. Memo loved Chinese food and when she visited, they drove to Los Angeles to visit Chinatown to have a real, authentic Chinese meal. Red loved his Grandmother and was proud of her, and the two of them had much fun together.

On the occasions that Ben and Liz visited the family took trips to Disneyland, the beaches and the many beautiful parks in the vicinity. Liz and Ben enjoyed the wonderful weather in the wintertime and were so thankful to be away from the cold and snow of Kentucky. Liz had expressed concern about earthquakes, and Becka prayed silently that none would happen while they were visiting, and, fortunately, none did.

Red was building up his accounting practice, and Becka was still not working, as Red was adamant that she stay at home with the children. Becka had secured a "Home Care License" and cared for other small children to supplement their income. She loved children, and Sherry and Davy liked the extra playmates.

But the money Becka made was not enough, and Red had taken the job as a fireman at Point Mugu Naval Air Test Center. The base was just south of Oxnard, and he was working there every other day in addition to his accounting practice. Soon, however, Red and Becka became acquainted with another young couple. Janie and Daren Wade had three little boys, and lived not far from them. Daren also worked in the accounting business, and even as Becka and Janie became good friends, Red and Daren decided to open an accounting practice together. They called their new practice "Wade and Duncan, Accountants"

The country was again involved in war. This time Red, although still in the Reserves, was not called up for service. His work at the fire department, and the fact that he was married with two small children, kept him from being called back into service as a fighter pilot. The war ended in stalemate, however. After more than three years of fighting, and at a loss of fifty three thousand Americans, (not including the wounded and missing) an armistice was signed to end the fighting. Once again, it was a terrible loss of lives, equipment, homes, and environment.

At the home place in Westview, Kentucky, Ben and

Liz were getting on with their lives and enjoying Ben's retirement. They made several trips to Falls Church to visit Maggie and John, and to get acquainted with their new little "adopted" grandson, Johnny. He was a sweet little boy with large brown eyes and curly brown hair, bright, and interested in everything around him.

Maggie continued to teach at the high school. A popular teacher; her classes in art, math and music were well attended. John, her husband, worked as a budget officer for the government and continued to take classes at Georgetown University in D.C, graduating with a degree in Business Administration.

Henry had returned home from the Service full of ambition to get a good job and get married. He found a great position as a metallurgist at the mill, and also became a part of Armco's public relations department. He soon asked his favorite girl, Helena to marry him. They were married soon after his return home and Ben and Liz helped them to build a small house near their own. Helena and Becka were pregnant at the same time, and their boys, Danny and Davy, were born within days of each other.

Later, Henry and Helena purchased a larger home that overlooked a beautiful valley. It was not far from Ben and Elizabeth's home, so they were able to see each other often.

Harry remained in the service and continued his medical studies, graduating as an M.D. When the Korean Conflict (as it was called) began, he was deployed there, working in a M.A.S.H. field hospital. After the end of the Conflict, he returned home and transferred to Pensacola, Florida, where he took a position as the Dean of a Community College. The author of many books, Harry continued to write for many years. He and his wife, Millie, had four children, twin boys,

Jamie and Jonnie, an older son, Stevie, and a pretty little dark haired girl, Peggy, who, according to Harry, resembled her Aunt Becka.

Becka kept in touch with all her family. She wrote often to her mother and dad, and wrote or called Harry and Henry. She kept up with Maggie and Will and their families. Will now had three daughters, and was working as an engineer helping to build nuclear reactor power plants. Although it was dangerous work, it was a well paying position, and Will really enjoyed what he did.

On one visit that Liz and Ben made to see Becka and her family, they decided to take a trip up the coast to see the giant redwood trees and other points of interest along the California coast. They started with a visit to Laguna Beach, and the Marine Corps Air Station at El Toro. From there they continued north to the La Brea Tar Pits in Los Angeles, to Hearst Castle on the central coast, and up through the Coastal Redwoods. Their journey carried them north as far as Eureka near the Oregon border before turning back south, there to visit Yosemite, Kings Canyon, and Sequoia National Park. It was their first long trip, ten days. They covered a lot of territory, and found sleeping in motels to be an adventure. But, everyone enjoyed it, especially the youngsters.

Sherry was six years old and Davy was almost three. On one occasion during the drive through the mountains, the children needed a potty break. There was no convenient place for them to take them, so they stopped beside the highway and let the kids relieve themselves. Davy had no trouble, but Sherry, unable to "aim" correctly, managed to wet her pretty white socks. Upon seeing the situation, Becka began scolding her for the infraction. But Sherry, after pulling up her panties, put her little hands on her hips.

"Well, for Pete's sake, Mommy," she said in a hurt voice, "I don't have a handy little thing like Davy has!" Then stamping her little foot to emphasize the point, she climbed back in the car.

Red, Hoss and Liz laughed heartily! Becka apologized to Sherry and said, "I hear you honey, and you've got a point."

"No" answered Sherry "I don't have a point like Davy's!"

The ride through the redwood trees was very exciting for the children as well as for the adults. Becka said that driving through those magnificent trees was almost like being in the loveliest cathedral in the world. The tall stately trees towered above them, seemingly brushing the sky with their branches. One giant had fallen but was still alive, its branches now growing up towards the sun. A road had been cut through the tree and the family drove Ben's beautiful long red Nash Ambassador Sedan right through it. Red had purchased a movie camera when Davy was only a baby, and had taken many home movies. The movies he took on this trip with Becka's parents became a "classic" for the whole family, and were shown over and over again.

During the times when Ben and Liz were able to stay in Ventura for the winter, they rented an apartment in The Seaview Inn, a large old Victorian home that overlooked the ocean.

Now that the children were older and in school every day, Becka had taken a job at the county courthouse as a clerk, and the job allowed Becka an hour for lunch. Ventura was located on a sloping plain overlooking the Pacific Ocean and a wide street ran down the hill from the courthouse to the beach. Liz and Ben's apartment in the Victorian was fairly close by, and although she and Red had purchased a second car, Becka would often walk down the hill to lunch with her parents on the Victorian's large, wide veranda. The veranda wrapped around the house, was partly glass, partly screened, and faced the ocean, the Channel Islands, and Ventura's nearly mile long pier. Sitting and watching the waves running up the beach below, Becka would often comment to her parents about their million dollar view! And during those wonderful "winters" Ben and Liz could often be seen walking on the beach, and fishing off the pier. On many occasions Liz and Ben would cook great dinners for Becka's family, or, just as frequently, drive to Becka's home in Montalvo to spend time with her family there.

Ben took advantage of the visits to Becka's home by making a great little workbench for Davy. It was about two feet high with brackets to hold all the small tools Davy would need for his "work." Davy loved the workbench and especially loved this great man he called "Hoss." He helped his grandpa work on an unfinished basement, and later used the area as a real workplace as he grew older. Ben also made hardwood headboards with shelves for books and lamps for Becka and Red's room, and, also for Sherry's room. Davy had bunk beds, and was happy with his work-table. And throughout it all, Becka and Red could often be seen capturing the happy moments on their small, 8 mm movie camera.

When Liz and Ben visited the little family, they attended a local Community church along with Becka. They became acquainted with many of the church members and Becka often hosted the Women's Group in her home. During one of these meetings Davy ran into the room and straight up to "Sister" Grossfield's chair.

"Have you seen my pet snake?" he asked sweetly. "I think I left him in your chair."

Sister Grossfield screamed and jumped out of the chair,

overturning it, and she, along with all the other women quickly ran out the door and into the sunny front yard! And, as Davy found the small green snake and put it back in its container in his room, Liz and Becka could not hide their laughter!

Liz was grateful to be away from the snow and ice, the slushy, miserable icy rain, and the generally bad weather of the Ohio Valley during the long, winter months. Because of this, Liz and Ben always planned their return home to coincide with spring when eastern Kentucky put on its most beautiful garments; tulips, marigolds, and buttercups, dogwood, and mountain laurel. And, they would arrive home in Ashland just in time to find the apple trees in full bloom. Liz and Ben, who had grown up in the East, felt there was no place as spectacularly beautiful as eastern Kentucky in the spring of the year, and Becka loved it, too.

But not every winter was spent in California. One winter Ben and Liz visited one of Ben's special friends who lived in Florida. While Ben enjoyed the visit, Liz wasn't crazy about it, having done all the housework for the friend, who was a widower.

"Cooking, washing clothes, and doing laundry isn't what I consider to be a vacation," she told Becka. "I don't mind doing the housework, but it seems to me that he just saves up the messes…all year, mind you…for me to clean once we get down there!"

And, the two experienced several severe storms in Florida as well. It seemed to Ben that his friend's home was right in the path of the storms. Twice, once in the fall after they got there, and once in the spring before they left for home, the storms were severe enough that everyone had to be evacuated. Of course, having grown up in the east, both Ben and Liz were used to lively weather, but these two particular wind and rainstorms were unbelievable. Their friend had damage to his roof, and many of his plants and trees were destroyed, but his home remained intact and the roof was quickly repaired…thanks to Ben's excellent knowledge of such things.

Regardless, Liz did not want to spend another winter in Florida. "But," she would amend, "we do enjoy visiting Harry and his family in Pensacola...and we do like the weather. Well...maybe a short trip to see Ben's friend."

Harry had a lovely home and he and his wife were always gracious hosts. Their children were lively and intelligent, and always made their grandparents feel special, but now, though, as they were growing older, Ben and Liz felt it best just to remain home, bad winters and all. During those winter months, Ben would set up the screen and get out the movies of their trips to California, Falls Church, and Florida. They would spend many long, dark evenings looking at the home movies. Liz would pop a big bowl of corn and Ben kept the fire in the fireplace burning brightly. The movie taken the year they rented the apartment in the old Victorian brought laughter at the shots showing Liz holding the big fish she'd caught while fishing on the pier in Ventura.

"Ben," Liz said to him one evening as they were preparing for bed, "Maggie called. She wants to plan a family reunion for next summer. She reminded me — as if I could forget — that it will be our 50th wedding anniversary! She wants to invite all the family to be here, and have a catered dinner served on the front lawn." Liz looked at Ben and smiled. "What do you think of her idea, honey?"

"Well," Ben drawled, "I reckon it would be alright." He got up and came to sit on the bed beside Liz. He put his arm around her and kissed her soft cheek. "You are as beautiful as you were 50 years ago…more beautiful really…and I love you even more now than I did then."

Ben was never demonstrative when others were present. Even his own children had seldom seen him hug or kiss their mother. Liz had told Maggie that Ben "made up for it when they were alone." She laughed at Maggie's expression, and with a twinkle in her eye she leaned down and squeezed Maggie's arm.

Maggie and her mother were very close, and as her parents grew older she spent more and more time with them. Liz was losing vision in one eye and had a heart murmur. Ben was, as he would say about himself, "as healthy as a working mule!" Liz's hair was now snow-white. Her beautiful eyes were still lovely and expressive and her face was lined with laugh lines. She had put on a few pounds, especially around her middle, but Ben called her plumpness "love handles" and told her he didn't want her to lose a single pound, he liked her just the way she was.

Ben was still straight as an arrow, with a full head of hair and very little gray showing only at the temples. He was a remarkably handsome man. When the two were together, they made a striking appearance.

Liz called Maggie and told her that she and Ben would be delighted to have a family reunion for their 50th anniversary. Maggie called all the family to let them know about the plans for that next summer. Becka, Harry, Henry, and Will and their families, all checked their calendars and planned to attend this important reunion.

There were many calls between Becka and Maggie that spring and early summer with the two planning the "big event" down to the last detail. They wanted it to be a special day for their parents. Collecting money from each family, they purchased a large golden fruit bowl, and had it engraved for the anniversary party. The year was 1962.

Becka and Red had recently moved into a lovely home in Ventura. It was near the college and located on a beautiful tree lined street. Sherry and Dave, both teenagers, were doing well in school, and Sherry would graduate from high school that spring. Dave would finish the ninth grade and start senior high in the fall of the year. They both played musical instruments. Dave contented himself with the sax. Sherry played both violin and piano, often playing for the church services on Sunday mornings.

The family attended church almost every Sunday. Both Dave and Sherry were involved with the youth groups at church, went to youth camps during the summer, and both played in the school orchestra and band.

Sherry was active in many school programs, the school paper, yearbook, assemblies, and so on. She loved school, and planned to attend the college near their home. Dave wanted to participate in sports programs such as football and baseball, and had a paper route that kept him very busy. He also loved to take long bike rides with his friends. Sometimes he was overjoyed to have his Dad accompany him. On these Saturdays they would take long rides throughout the surrounding groves and fields of growing vegetables that made up much of the countryside around Ventura County. There was a beautiful golf course near their home, and Red, an excellent golfer and enjoying this outdoor sport, often took Dave with him.

Red and his partner were doing well in the accounting business. The Wades lived nearby and their three teenage boys were also growing up fast. Janie Wade and Becka enjoyed each other's company and the two families sometimes had picnics at the local parks. At these outings Sherry often prevailed on her parents to allow her to bring a girlfriend, as she felt decidedly out numbered by all the boys! She was growing into a lovely young woman, with long dark blonde hair, big blue eyes and a lovely figure. She was about 5 feet 7 inches tall and had many "boy friends." She had been voted "The Girl Of The Year" at her high school, and was quite popular with both girls and boys.

There had been many trips to Kentucky over the years and the whole family was looking forward to the big reunion! Helena and Becka were good friends, ferquently shopping together and enjoying the children. Helena, a gracious hostess, always made Becka and her family feel welcome and loved. The summer before, Will's oldest daughter, Darla, had introduced Sherry to a handsome "hunk" named Charlie. Sherry hoped she'd see him again during her visit to Kentucky. Helena, Henry's wife, had obtained passes for Sherry and Dave to go with her sons to the large private swim club while they were visiting. A big adventure for the summer fun days, Dave and Sherry always had a lot of fun with Henry's boys, Dan and Daryl, as the four of them loved to swim.

On their drive back Red and Becka had managed to visit a number of National Parks during the children's growing up years. Among them, the Grand Canyon, and Carlsbad Caverns were among the favorites. During the years when Red's work didn't allow him to go, Becka would drive the children to Kentucky alone, again visiting the national parks along the way. She had no problem driving, and enjoyed these trips–she was determined that her children should know their grandparents, their cousins, and their aunts and uncles.

Becka also managed to visit Red's mother and stepfather, and to meet his half-brother, Richard. They lived in a beautiful area of Arkansas, and owned a small cattle ranch. Red's stepfather was a doctor who worked at a large hospital in Booneville, Arkansas. Both children loved the area and enjoyed their small cousin Lori, a lovely little girl with long hair and sparkling eyes.

Now, in this year of 1962, as the summer vacation approached, Red was not sure that he would be able to make the trip with the family. He didn't want them to miss going however, so he tried to arrange his time so he would be able to drive them there. As it turned out, his partner, Darin Wade was able to fill in for him and Red was happy to make the trip with the family.

Red and Becka were finding it difficult to travel with teenagers. The two fussed and complained, and generally made life miserable. Red had little patience with this kind of behavior, but Becka managed to get things on a happier basis by suggesting rest stops and snacks. It worked most every time. However, generally they enjoyed each other and had fun together, arriving at Ben and Liz's home several days before the planned reunion.

Ben and Liz were so happy to see them. Liz had the house all ready for their visit, with plenty of room for all. The old frame house had a new sparkling coat of white paint, the bedrooms had been re-wallpapered, the garden was full of flowers, and many of the apple trees still had apples to pick. Liz had purchased new linens, tablecloths, and colorful towels and had vases of flowers throughout the house. Becka hugged her mother and remarked that the house and gardens had never looked so lovely!

Maggie, John and young Johnny were there, along with Henry and Harry and their families, Will and his family, as well as Henry's family lived nearby and planned to open their homes to out of town relatives. On the "big day" the entire group gathered on the front lawn. The weather cooperated with the sun smiling on them all. The grand kids enjoyed each other and had a great time. Will's youngest daughter, Billie, was the darling of the older grand children. She had just learned to walk and was interested in all the activities. Her big eyes missed nothing, and her happy laugh was contagious.

A cool breeze moved across the newly mowed lawns, the food was delicious, and everything went as Maggie and Becka had planned. Red hugged Liz and told her he was glad to see two of her famous apple pies on the picnic table! Then, with Ben and Liz standing behind the beautifully decorated anniversary cake, Red began taking pictures. Brothers and sisters, parents and children; many combinations of family portraits would be produced that day.

It was a large, happy, boisterous gathering, with laughter, music and much fun. Becka, standing off to one side surveyed the noisy, happy group. She looked at Harry's smiling handsome face, at Henry–so much like Harry, but different, with his own persona. And she looked at Will, now growing a little bald, but with twinkling eyes and teasing fun. She caught a glimpse of Maggie, scurrying in and out of the house, bringing this and that to the long table, now "groaning" with the weight of all kinds of food!

John, Maggie's husband was seated to one side, smoking a large cigar and grinning at the kids, who scampered here and there. Becka looked over at her Mom and Dad sitting in the large wooden lawn chairs and watching the grandkids as they chased each other around the lawns. Liz's body shook with laughter.

For a moment Becka felt Bart's presence near her. She closed her eyes and could see his smiling face. A tear slid down her cheek.

Red quietly joined her. "Hey, little Dolly," he said softly, "what are the tears for?" Putting his arm around her he gave her a gentle hug.

"Oh, Red, I guess I'm just crying for happiness!" Becka Snuggling close to her husband and feeling his warmth, she was so happy that he had been able to come for this very special time. And suddenly she remembered a dream she'd had several months before…a dream in which she saw her mother walking with Bart and Will…and the three were smiling and talking together…and Liz's mother, Sarah was there also…then the dream gradually faded into the familiar mist that so often shrouded these dreams.

Standing apart with Red, Becka watched the happy children at play, her parents laughing and enjoying all the festivities. She watched Maggie as she ran in and out of the house, smiling and teasing the children as they ate watermelon and spit out the seeds. Becka's heart swelled with love for Maggie and appreciation for all the many things she did to keep the family close, knowing it was mainly through her sister's efforts that they were all gathered here on this lovely summer day. Now, looking around, Becka was filled with love for them all.

Putting all feelings of forebodings to the back of her mind, she walked with Red to the table for some more fried chicken (and another piece of apple pie for Red), and both poured themselves hot coffee.

Dave and Danny, along with little Daryl ran to ask if they could have more ice cream. Will's older daughters Darla and Rita with Sherry had a lively game of badminton going on the side lawn. Steve, Harry's oldest son was pestering the older girls, and trying to get in on the game. Little Peggy and Will's youngest daughter Billie, sat on the lawn, playing with the dog.

Family Reunion
Summer 1962

Liz leaned across the arm of the lawn chair and squeezing Ben's arm and whispered into his ear, "Just look, Ben. Look at what we started fifty years ago!" And tears of happiness filled her eyes as she looked at all of her grandchildren…and her own children and Ben, her wonderful husband. Silently, Liz thanked God for all of these many blessings.

Their 50th reunion was a very, very, happy day!!

ELIZABETH'S OWN APPLE PIE

7 to 8 med. tart apples
1 tsp. cinnamon
1 full cup of sugar pinch of nutmeg
2 tablespoons of flour
2 tablespoons real butter
Pinch of salt
1 recipe plain pastry

PARE APPLES and slice thin, add sugar, salt flour and spices, blend. Fill 9-inch pie shell with apples that have been mixed with sugar flour and spices, dot with butter, arrange the top crust evenly over apples, crimp edges, and brush top of pie with a mixture of melted butter and cinnamon. With a sharp knife carve an A on the top crust.

Note: If apples are not tart, add 1 tablespoon of lemon juice to mixture before filling pie shell. Bake in hot oven (400) for 10 minutes; reduce heat to (350) and bake an additional 40 to 45 minutes, until top crust is golden brown, and apples are done.

AUTHOR'S NOTE

MANY OF the events and episodes in this book are taken from real life and are true, although fictionalized for better comprehension. Some of the names and places have been changed. As a memoir or chronicle of a family during momentous changes in our country's history, this book endeavors to record their responses to these changes; in war and tragedy, in humor and in mystery, but above all, in their faith in and love for each other.

ACKNOWLEDGEMENTS

I WISH FIRST of all to thank my parents, for much of this is really their story. Also I sincerely thank my brothers Jack and Bill, and my sister, Frances, all of whom have passed through the veil, but whose spirits I feel with me. Many thanks to my youngest brother Bob who served his country during World War Two, fighting on the battlefields of Europe, and enduring close, violent combat in France and Germany. Bob was very helpful in jogging my memory about childhood escapades, as well as some of his own experiences during World War Two.

To my first husband, and the father of my children. Warren "Red" Duncan, was part of "The Greatest Generation,"* and served with valor during World War Two.

(He passed through "the veil" in 1995.)

To my children Sharon and Dave who encouraged me to "keep on writing," and, for their excellent editorial help.

Special thanks to my husband, Raymond for his wonderful patience, love, and encouragement. His help has been invaluable.

May God bless you all.

---

* *The Greatest Generation* by Tom Brokaw, 1998 Random House

The author may be contacted by email at
RBLG 337 @ yahoo .com

www.ingramcontent.com/pod-product-compliance
Ingram Content Group UK Ltd.
Pitfield, Milton Keynes, MK11 3LW, UK
UKHW041948190726
13854UKWH00004B/1861

9 781412 085519